Understanding Finance

Understanding Finance

ROBERT LEACH

MERCURY

First published in 1991
by Mercury Books
Gold Arrow Publications Limited, 862 Garratt Lane, London SW17 0NB

Set in Palatino by Phoenix Photosetting, Chatham, Kent
Printed and bound in Great Britain by
Mackays of Chatham PLC, Chatham, Kent

British Library Cataloguing in Publication Data
Leach, Robert *1949 Nov. 19*
  Understanding finance.
  1. Finance
  I. Title
  332

  ISBN 1-85252-028-0

CONTENTS

PREFACE

Money is something which concerns all of us, yet very few of us begin to understand many of its complexities. This book attempts to provide an introduction to such areas.

It cannot be completely comprehensive. That would require a set of encyclopaedias. But I hope it will give an overview of some of the more important areas.

The book introduces you to some basic economic ideas, to taxes, insurance, pensions and financial planning. It explains some of the factors surrounding interest rates and inflation. It gives you some basic legal understanding of hire purchase and employment.

I hope that you find the book interesting and useful.

Robert Leach
Epsom, December 1990

1

CURRENCY AND LEGAL TENDER

1.1 Currency

The currency in the UK is the pound sterling. Since 'decimal day', 15 February 1971, the pound sterling has been divided into 100 pence. The pound is denoted by the symbol £ placed before the number; the pence are denoted by the letter p after the number. The £ symbol is a form of the letter L from *librum*, the Latin word for 'pound'.

Large amounts are often indicated in thousands, millions or billions of pounds thus:

£28,000   £28m   £28bn

or in a table:

£'000	£m	£bn
28	28	28

Before 15 February 1971, the pound was divided into 20 shillings, each of which was divided into 12 (old) pence. A quarter of an old penny was a farthing. For 18 months after decimal day, both the old and new systems were used side by side, though most people switched to decimal currency as soon as possible. The old currency was denoted thus: £6 2s 4d. Amounts less than £1 were usually denoted in the form 4/9 or 5/-, though 4s 9d and 5s 0d were the 'proper' forms.

The 'guinea' is £1.05. It has never been an officially used measure but was commonly used before decimalisation, since when it has effectively died out.

[1]

1.2 Legal tender

Legal tender comprises banknotes and coins which are used as the everyday currency.

Coins and notes have a different legal status, which reflects their history. A coin is a token (now only issued by the Royal Mint) which has the status of legal tender by an Act of Parliament (currently Coinage Act 1971). The original coins were pieces of precious metal bearing an official stamp to verify their weight and size but whose value was determined by the value of the metal, an idea reintroduced by the Britannia coin.

Banknotes are promissory notes issued by the Bank of England and three Scottish banks. Their status as legal tender derives from the common law. They were originally receipts given by the bank for deposits of gold.

Scotland and England use the same coins but have different banknotes. English banknotes are legal tender in Scotland. Scottish banknotes are not strictly legal tender in England, though in practice they are regarded as legal tender, and will be accepted by English banks.

In the UK a surprisingly large number of notes and coins are legal tender. Many coins, however, are rarely, if ever, used as legal tender, as they have a much higher value to a coin collector. These rare items are shown below in square brackets.

The complete range of legal tender comprises:

£100	banknote issued by Bank of Scotland
£100	banknote issued by Royal Bank of Scotland
£100	banknote issued by Clydesdale Bank
[£100	Britannia 1oz gold coin, first minted 1986]
£50	banknote issued by Bank of England, first issued 20 March 1981
£50	banknote issued by Clydesdale Bank
[£50	Britannia ½oz gold coin, first minted 1986]
[£25	Britannia ¼oz gold coin, first minted 1986]
£20	banknote issued by Bank of England, first issued 9 July 1970
£20	banknote issued by Bank of Scotland

£20	banknote issued by Royal Bank of Scotland
£20	banknote issued by Clydesdale Bank
£10	banknote issued by Bank of England, first issued 20 February 1975
£10	banknote issued by Bank of Scotland
£10	banknote issued by Royal Bank of Scotland
£10	banknote issued by Clydesdale Bank
[£10	Britannia $\frac{1}{10}$oz gold coin, first minted 1986]
£5	banknote issued by Bank of England, first issued 11 November 1971
£5	banknote issued by Bank of Scotland
£5	banknote issued by Royal Bank of Scotland
£5	banknote issued by Clydesdale Bank
[£5	crown to celebrate the Queen Mother's birthday, minted in 1990]
[£5	gold coin, if minted since 1887]
£2	coin minted in 1986 and 1989
[£2	gold coin, if minted since 1887]
£1	coin, minted from 1983
£1	banknote issued by Bank of Scotland
£1	banknote issued by Royal Bank of Scotland
£1	banknote issued by Clydesdale Bank
[£1	gold sovereign, if minted since 1838]
50p	coin, first minted in 1969
[50p	gold half sovereign, if minted since 1838]
[25p	crowns, if minted since 1816]
20p	coin, first minted in 1982
[20p	silver double florin, minted between 1887 and 1890]
10p	coin, first minted in 1968
10p	florin, minted between 1816 and 1967
5p	coin, first minted in 1968
5p	shilling, if minted between 1816 and 1967
[4p	Maundy coin, if minted since 1816]
[3p	Maundy coin, if minted since 1816]
2p	coin, first minted in 1971
[2p	Maundy coin, if minted since 1816]
1p	coin, first minted in 1971
[1p	Maundy coin, if minted since 1816]

The £1 note as first issued by the Bank of England on 9

[3]

February 1978 was withdrawn from 1984 and ceased to be legal tender on 11 March 1988.

A new 5p coin was introduced in June 1990, and a new 10p coin will be in June 1992. These coins are smaller than the previous 5p and 10p coins.

The current range of banknotes is also being replaced with the E Series starting with the £5 note in 1990. Each new note will be smaller than the previous note.

Maundy money minted before 1971 was denominated in old pence. These coins are now legal tender for the same number of new pence – the only occasion on which the face value of a British coin has changed value after issue.

To stop people using large numbers of low value coins to settle bills, coins below £1 in value are only legal tender to these limits:

50p coins to £10
20p coins to £10
10p coins to £5
5p coins to £5
2p coins to 20p
1p coins to 20p

The banks will accept coins to any value. However, if the coins are not bagged up properly, heavy charges may be made for doing so.

1.3 Other British currency

The Republic of ireland produces its own notes and coins. These ceased to be legal tender on 30 March 1979, when the Irish pound, known as a punt and denominated IR£, floated against the pound sterling. It is now treated exactly the same as any other foreign currency, and has been consistently worth less than a pound sterling.

The Channel Islands of Jersey and Guernsey each produce their own notes and coins, as does the Isle of Man. They have the same values as their UK counterparts but are not legal tender in the UK. UK banks will accept banknotes at face value but will not accept coins.

[4]

The Island of Lundy in the Bristol Channel illegally issued a coin known as the 'puffin' in 1929 and a spurious proof set in 1965.

1.4 Old notes and coins

When a note or coin ceases to be legal tender it is said to be 'demonetised'. Even though it is no longer legal tender, an old UK banknote or coin never loses its value. Old banknotes can always be exchanged for current notes at the Bank of England (or Scottish banks). This is usually arranged through a local bank. The legend 'I promise to pay bearer on demand . . .' is the guarantee that the banknote will always be honoured. Despite what many people believe, the right to receive gold to the value of a banknote was finally abolished as long ago as 1935.

Old coins will be exchanged by the Royal Mint for new coins provided each value of old coin is submitted in amounts of at least £1.

Demonetised banknotes are:

- £1,000, £500, £300, £200, £100, £50, £40, £30, £25 and £15 'black and white' notes issued by the Bank of England from 1745, demonetised on 1 May 1945.
- £10 'black and white' notes issued from 1759, demonetised on 1 May 1945.
- £5 blue note with the Queen's portrait issued from 1963, demonetised on 1 September 1973.
- £5 blue note with a picture of Britannia issued from 1957, demonetised on 27 June 1967.
- £5 'black and white' note with straight edge issued from 1945, demonetised on 14 March 1961.
- £5 'black and white' note issued from 1793, demonetised from 1 March 1946.
- £1 green note issued from 1955, demonetised on 11 March 1988.
- £1 green note issued before 1955, demonetised on 29 May 1962.
- £1 blue note issued in 1940, demonetised on 29 May 1962.

- 10 shilling (50p) note issued from 1961, demonetised on 21 November 1970.
- 10 shilling note issued before 1961, demonetised on 30 October 1962.

Before 15 February 1971 'silver' coins were legal tender if minted from 1816 and 'copper' coins if minted from 1860. Demonetised coins from this period are:

- 2s 6d (12½p) half-crowns minted to 1967, demonetised on 1 January 1970.
- 6d (2½p) coin minted to 1967, demonetised on 1 July 1980.
- 3d (1¼p) 12-sided coin minted between 1937 and 1967, demonetised on 1 September 1971.
- 3d (1¼p) silver coin minted between 1834 and 1944, demonetised on 1 September 1971.
- ½p coin minted between 1971 and 1984, demonetised on 1 January 1985.
- 1d (0.417p) coin minted to 1967, demonetised on 1 September 1971.
- ½d (0.208p) coin minted to 1967, demonetised on 1 August 1969.
- ¼d (0.104p) farthing minted to 1956, demonetised on 1 January 1961.

Although coins are still referred to as silver and copper, 'silver' coins have been made from cupro-nickel since 1947 and 'copper' coins have been made from bronze since 1860.

1.5 Consequences of legal tender

The main purpose of legal tender is that you must not refuse it in settlement of a debt. If someone who owes you money offers it to you in legal tender and you refuse to accept it, that person may be able to argue that the debt is extinguished and he no longer owes you the money. You do not have to give change, accept a cheque or a credit card, or accept coins above their maximum tender value. In England you do not have to accept Scottish banknotes.

In practice most people will usually give change, accept

Scottish notes or accept a cheque against a cheque card. You are free to accept whatever you like in settlement of a debt, and this may include foreign coins, coupons, tokens, credit cards, bills of exchange, postage stamps, postal orders, jewellery or almost anything else.

Another consequence of legal tender is that there are strict laws governing forgery of such items. It is an offence to forge items or to sell forgeries at less than face value. It is also an offence to keep a forgery or forging equipment without lawful excuse. The Bank of England takes a very hard line on this, even stopping people using designs similar to banknotes on aprons and tea-towels. However, it failed to get a prosecution brought against an artist who drew copies of banknotes.

Legal tender status also tends to make the notes and coins more valuable to collectors.

1.6 Damaged notes and coins

Damaged and defaced notes and coins remain legal tender while they are still recognisable.

Damaged banknotes may be exchanged for new notes at the Post Office provided:

1   at least half the note is present,
2   it is not in more than four pieces,
3   the legend 'I promise to pay bearer the sum of' is wholly present,
4   there is at least one complete banknote number, and
5   there is at least one-third of the chief cashier's signature.

If the banknote is more damaged, it can be exchanged at the Bank of England, usually by handling it in with a completed form at a local bank. It is known that the Bank of England has been able to replace even notes which have been reduced to pulp in a washing machine.

1.7 Other ways of making payment

Payment in cash is not always convenient. It is expensive and inconvenient to carry or send large amounts, there is always a security risk, and you have no automatic record. For this reason many other ways of making payment have been developed:

1 postal orders and money orders,
2 cheques,
3 bills of exchange,
4 bank transfers, and
5 plastic money.

Postal orders are discussed in section 1.8. Other methods of payment are discussed in chapter 7.

Sometimes you buy goods or services in two stages. For example, you buy postage stamps and then use those stamps to pay for your postage. Another example is buying a phonecard, which you then use to pay for your telephone calls.

You may not always have the money to buy what you want when you want. If not, you may borrow from a bank or a finance company. These arrangements are explained in chapters 7 and 8.

1.8 Postal orders and money orders

Postal orders are usually used to send small amounts by post. They can be bought from any post office for these amounts: 25p, 30p, 35p, 40p, 45p, 50p, 60p, 70p, 75p, 80p, 90p, £1, £2, £3, £4, £5, £6, £7, £8, £9, £10, £20. Their value may be increased by up to 9p by adding one or two postage stamps.

There is a charge for supplying a postal order, known as poundage. This is currently 20p for postal orders up to £1 in value, and 30p above. If a post office has run out of the particular value wanted, the post office will supply two or more orders to the value requested for the same poundage as if one postal order had been supplied.

Each postal order has a counterfoil, a piece which you can tear off. You can ask the post-office counter clerk to stamp the counterfoil, so that you have a record of when and where you bought it.

The postal order may be either 'open' or 'crossed'. It will

be given to you as an open postal order. You cross it yourself by drawing two parallel lines across it. An open postal order may be cashed at a post office or paid into a bank account. A crossed postal order may only be paid into a bank account. If you wish, you can write the name of a bank between the parallel lines; the postal order can then only be paid into an account at that bank.

The postal order has spaces for you to write the name of the person who are sending the money to (known as the 'payee') and an address. If you leave this blank, anyone finding the postal order may cash it at any post office. If you write in a person's name, only that person may cash it. The address must be that of a post office, not the payee's own address. If you write in an address, the payee can only cash the postal order at that post office. If you just write a town, village or district, the postal order may be cashed at any post office in that place.

If you receive an unaddressed postal order, you should write your name on it immediately to stop someone else cashing it. If you receive an uncrossed postal order which you wish to pay into a bank account, you should cross it on receipt.

Postal orders remain valid for 6 months from the end of the month in which it was issued. So a postal order issued on 10 February 1990 is valid until 31 August 1990.

The person who bought the postal order in the first place may obtain a refund from the post office by presenting the postal order and the counterfoil at a post office. The poundage will not be refunded.

Postal orders cannot be negotiated as cheques can. That means if you receive a postal order payable to you for £10, you cannot sign it over to someone to whom you owe £10.

If a postal order is cashed by someone not entitled to cash it, the rightful owner may be able to claim compensation from the Post Office, depending on the circumstances. If a postal order is lost in the post, the Post Office will pay compensation only if the postal order was crossed or had the payee's name on it or was sent by registered post.

A few other countries pay or issue (or both) British postal orders.

1.9 Foreign currency

Different countries of the world have their own currencies. Table 1.1 lists the countries, their currencies, the usual abbreviation, and how they are divided.

TABLE 1.1   Foreign currencies

Country	Unit	Abbr.	Smaller unit
Afghanistan	afghani	Af	= 100 puli
Albania	lek	Lk	= 100 qindars
Algeria	Algerian dinar	AD	= 100 centimes
Andorra	French franc	Fr	= 100 centimes
Angola	kwanza	Kw	= 100 cents
Antigua	E. Caribbean dollar	ECar$	= 100 cents
Argentina	austral	Aus	= 100 centavos
Australia	Australian dollar	A$	= 100 cents
Austria	Schilling	Sch	= 100 groschen
Bahamas	Bahamian dollar	Ba$	= 100 cents
Bahrain	Bahraini dinar	BD	= 1,000 fils
Bangladesh	taka	Tk	= 100 poisha
Barbados	Barbados dollar	Bds$	= 100 cents
Belgium	Belgian franc	Bf	= 100 centimes
Belize	Belize dollar	B$	= 100 cents
Benin	CFA franc	CFA Fr	= 100 centimes
Bermuda	Bermuda dollar	Bda$	= 100 cents
Bhutan	ngultrum	N	= 2 tikchung
			= 100 Indian paise
Bolivia	boliviano	B$	= 100 centavos
Botswana	pula	Pu	= 100 cents
Brazil	cruzado	Cr	= 100 centavos
Brunei	Brunei dollar	Br$	= 100 cents
Bulgaria	lev	Lv	= 100 stotinki
Burkino Faso	CFA franc	CFA Fr	= 100 centimes
Burma	kyat	Kt	= 100 pyas
Burundi	Burundi franc	BFr	= 100 centimes
Cameroon	CFA franc	CFA Fr	= 100 centimes
Canada	Canadian dollar	Can$	= 100 cents
Cape Verde Is.	Cape Verde escudo	CV Esc	= 100 centavos
Cayman Islands	Cayman Is. dollar	Cay I$	= 100 cents

Central African Republic	CFA franc	CFA Fr	= 100 cents
Chad	CFA franc	CFA Fr	= 100 cents
Chile	Chilean peso	Ch$	= 100 centavos
China	yuan	Y	= 10 chiao or jiao = 100 fen
Colombia	Colombian peso	Col$	= 100 centavos
Congo	CFA franc	CFA Fr	= 100 centimes
Cuba	Cuban peso	Cub$	= 100 centavos
Cyprus	Cyprus pound	C£	= 1,000 mils
Czechoslovakia	koruna	Kcs	= 100 haleru
Denmark	krone	DKr	= 100 örer
Djibouti	Djibouti franc	DjFr	= 100 centimes
Dominica	E. Caribbean dollar	ECar$	= 100 cents
Dominican Rep.	Dominican Republic dollar	DR$	= 8 reales = 100 centavos
Ecuador	sucre	Su	= 100 centavos
Egypt	Egyptian pound	E$	= 100 piastres = 100 millièmes
El Salvador	El Salvador colón	ESC	= 100 centavos
Equatorial Guinea	ekpwele, or CFA franc	E CFA Fr	= 100 céntimos = 100 centimes
Ethiopia	birr	Br	= 100 cents
Falkland Is.	Falkland Is. pound	Fl£	= 100 pence
Fiji	Fiji dollar	F$	= 100 cents
Finland	Finnish mark	F Mk	= 100 pennia
France	French franc	Fr	= 100 centimes
French Guinea	French franc	Fr	= 100 centimes
Gabon	CFA franc	CFA Fr	= 100 centimes
Gambia	dalasi	Di	= 100 butut
Germany	Deutschemark	DM	= 100 pfennig
Ghana	cedi	C	= 100 pesewas
Gibraltar	Gibraltar pound	Gib£	= 100 pence
Greece	drachma	Dr	= 100 lepta
Greenland	kroner	DKr	= 100 örer
Grenada	E. Caribbean dollar	ECar$	= 100 cents
Guatemala	quetzal	Q	= 100 centavos
Guinea	syli franc	Sy	= 100 cauris
Guinea-Bissau	Guinea-Bissau peso	GB P	= 100 centavos
Guyana	Guyana dollar	Guy$	= 100 cents

[11]

TABLE 1.1   Foreign currencies – *cont*

Country	Unit	Abbr.	Smaller unit
Haiti	gourde	Gde	= 100 centimes
Honduras	lempira	La	= 100 centavos
Hong Kong	Hong Kong dollar	HK$	= 100 cents
Hungary	forint	Ft	= 100 filler
Iceland	Icelandic króna	IKr	= 100 aurar
India	Indian rupee	Re	= 100 paise
Indonesia	rupiah	Rp	= 100 sen
Iran	rial	RI	= 100 dinars
Iraq	Iraqi dollar	ID	= 1,000 fils
Ireland	punt	IR£	= 100 pence
Israel	new shekel	IS	= 100 new agorot
Italy	lira	L	= 100 centesimi
Ivory Coast	CFA franc	CFA fr	= 100 centimes
Jamaica	Jamaican dollar	Jam$	= 100 cents
Japan	yen	Y	= 100 sen
Jordan	Jordanian dollar	JD	= 1,000 fils
Kampuchea	riel	CRI	= 100 sen
Kenya	Kenyan shilling	KSh	= 100 cents
Korea, North	North Korean won	NK W	= 100 jon
Korea, South	S Korean won-hwan	SK W	= 100 chon
Kuwait	Kuwait dinar	KD	= 1,000 fils
Laos	kip poy po	Kp	= 100 at
Lebanon	Lebanese pound	L£	= 100 piastres
Lesotho	loti	L	= 100 lisente
Liberia	Liberian dollar	L$	= 100 cents
Libya	Libyan dinar	LD	= 1,000 dirhams
Liechtenstein	Swiss franc	SFr	= 100 centimes
Luxembourg	Luxembourg franc	LFr	= 100 centimes
Malagasy Rep.	Malagasy franc	MalFr	= 100 centimes
Malawi	Malawi kwacha	Mk	= 100 tambala
Malaysia	ringgit	M$	= 100 cents
Maldives	Ruflyra	MvRe	= 100 paise
Mali	CFA franc	CFA Fr	= 100 centimes
Malta	Maltese pound	M£	= 100 cents
			= 1,000 mils

[12]

Currency and Legal Tender

Mauritania	ouguiya	U	= 5 khoums
Mauritius	Mauritian rupee	MauR	= 100 cents
Mexico	Mexican peso	Mex$	= 100 centavos
Monaco	French franc	Fr	= 100 centimes
Mongolia	tugrik	Tug	= 100 möngös
Morocco	dirham	Dh	= 100 centimes
Mozambique	metical	M	= 100 centavos
Namibia	rand	R	= 100 cents
Nauru	Australian dollar	A$	= 100 cents
Nepal	Nepalese rupee	NRe	= 100 paise
Netherlands	guilder	Gld	= 100 cents
Netherlands Antilles	Antillian guilder	AGld	= 100 cents
New Zealand	New Zealand dollar	NZ$	= 100 cents
Nicaragua	córdoba	C	= 100 centavos
Niger	CFA franc	CFA Fr	= 100 cents
Nigeria	naira	N	= 100 kobo
Norway	krone	NKr	= 100 örer
Oman	rial Omani	RO	= 1,000 biazes
Pakistan	Pakistan rupee	PakRe	= 100 paise
Panama	balboa	Ba	= 100 centésimos
Papua New Guinea	kina	Ka	= 100 toea
Paraguay	guarani	G	= 100 centimos
Peru	inti	S	= 100 centavos
Philippines	Philippines peso	PP	= 100 centavos
Poland	zloty	Zl	= 100 groszy
Portugal	escudo	Esc	= 100 centavos
Puerto Rico	US dollar	$	= 100 cents
Qatar	Qatar riyal	QR	= 100 dirhams
Romania	leu	leu	= 100 bani
Rwanda	Rwanda franc	RwFr	= 100 centimes
Saudi Arabia	Saudi riyal	SA R	= 100 halalah
Senegal	CFA franc	CFA Fr	= 100 centimes
Seychelles	Seychelles rupee	S Re	= 100 cents
Sierra Leone	leone	Le	= 100 cents
Singapore	Singapore dollar	Sing$	= 100 cents
Somalia	Somali shilling	SoSh	= 100 cents

[13]

TABLE 1.1   Foreign currencies – *cont*

Country	Unit	Abbr.	Smaller unit
South Africa	rand	R	= 100 cents
Spain	peseta	Pt	= 100 centimos
Sri Lanka	Sri Lanka rupee	SL Re	= 100 cents
Sudan	Sudanese pound	Sud£	= 100 piastres
Surinam	Surinam guilder	S Gld	= 100 cents
Swaziland	lilangeni	Li	= 100 cents
Sweden	krona	S Kr	= 100 örer
Switzerland	Swiss franc	SFr	= 100 centimes
Syria	Syrian pound	S£	= 100 piastres
Taiwan	Taiwan dollar	T$	= 100 cents
Tanzania	Tanzanian shilling	TSh	= 100 cents
Thailand	baht	Bt	= 100 satang
Togo	CFA franc	CFA Fr	= 100 centimes
Trinidad and Tobago	Trinidad and Tobago dollar	TT$	= 100 cents
Tunisia	dinar	TD	= 1,000 millimes
Turkey	Turkish lira	TL	= 100 kurus
Uganda	new shilling	USh	= 100 cents
UAE	UAE dirham	UAE Dh	= 100 fils
UK	pound	£	= 100 pence
USA	dollar	$	= 100 cents
USSR	rouble	Rub	= 100 kopecks
Uruguay	Uruguay new peso	UN$	= 100 centésimos
Venezuela	bolivar	B	= 100 céntimos
Vietnam	dong	D	= 10 hao = 100 xu
Western Samoa	tala	WS$	= 100 cents
Yemen, North	rial	YR	= 100 fils
Yemen, South	South Yemeni dinar	YD	= 1,000 fils
Yugoslavia	Yugoslav dinar	YuD	= 100 paras
Zaire	zaire	Z	= 100 makuta
Zambia	kwacha	K	= 100 ngwee
Zimbabwe	Zimbabwean dollar	Z$	= 100 cents

The following currency changes have occurred since 1980:

1 Argentina changed from the peso to the austral on 15 June 1985.
2 Bolivia changed from the peso to the boliviano on 1 January 1987.
3 Brazil changed from the cruzeiro to the cruzado on 1 March 1986.
4 Iceland changed from the old króna to the new króna (= 100 old króna) on 1 January 1981.
5 Israel changed from the pound to the shekel on 24 February 1980 (1S = £10), and from the shekel to the new shekel on 3 September 1985.
6 Peru changed from the sol to the inti on 1 January 1986.

1.10 Exchange control

To stop money leaving a country, a government sometimes imposes exchange control regulations. These either limit the amount of money which may leave the country, or keep the exchange rate for the currency artificially high.

The UK, like most countries, had strict control on the export of capital from the 1930s. In the UK this took the form of the Exchange Control Act 1948. This Act was suspended in 1979 and finally abolished in 1987. Between those years it was used only once, to restrict capital movements with Argentina during the Falklands war of 1982.

When one currency is physically changed to another, it is said to be 'converted'. If an amount is simply expressed in another currency, it is said to be 'translated'.

The rates usually quoted are the average of the buying and selling rates. There is a whole range of different rates quoted for different purposes. The banks will give you less foreign currency when selling it than when buying it (and charge you commission for doing so). Many countries have different rates for different transactions. Some countries (e.g. Spain) distinguish internal currency from external.

The current exchange rates between banks are known as

'spot rates', which will be subject to a premium or discount for buying currency at a future date. Where two countries each trade in the other's currency, it is possible for them to offer slightly different rates.

Details on other currencies as an economic measure are given in section 3.10.

1.11 International currency

In addition to the actual currencies of the world, various international currencies have been invented. The commonest of these now are the European Currency Unit (ecu) and Special Drawing Rights (SDRs).

The ecu is a creature of the EEC.

On 13 March 1979 the EEC formally established the European Monetary System (EMS) colloquially known as 'the snake'. The nickname refers to the fact that the currencies are connected but can 'wriggle' within limits. All EEC countries, including the UK, are members of EMS. The UK joined the Exchange Rate Mechanism (ERM) on 8 October 1990. The ERM limits the range by which EEC currencies may vary from a central rate.

The ecu is defined as a weighted average of all EEC currencies (including sterling). EMS members' currencies must keep to within 2.25 per cent of their agreed band, except that before 1990 the Italian lira was allowed 6 per cent (and there are concessions for Spain and the UK). EEC accounting is done in the unit of the ecu. In recent years it has also been possible for individuals to hold bank accounts in ecus, and in 1987 Belgium minted ecu coins. Neither of these last two innovations have really caught on. The ecu is worth about 70p.

The ecu should be distinguished from the écu, a name used for three different old French coins: a silver coin roughly equivalent to the English crown, a gold coin weighing 60 grains, and (colloquially) the 5-franc piece.

Special drawing rights are a creation of the International Monetary Fund. They were created in 1969 by the 'Group of Ten' (countries) as an economic tool to replace the previous reliance on dollars, sterling and gold as international cur-

[16]

rency standards. To December 1971 the SDR was worth $1, but after US devaluation in 1971 the rate became 1 SDR = $1.08571. Since 1974 it has floated with other currencies.

Other EEC phenomena such as *Eurodollars* and *Euroyen* do not represent a new currency so much as an existing currency held under particular circumstances.

The *green pound* is used as the unit for the Common Agricultural Policy (CAP) of the EEC. It is an ecu value but more narrowly defined.

The *French gold franc* is used as a measure for settling claims for lost aircraft baggage under a convention originally drafted in 1929. The rate is 250 French gold francs per kilo of cargo and 5,000 francs per passenger for luggage under the Warsaw–Hague Convention (in the UK the Carriage by Air Act 1961). When the Montreal agreement of 1975 is finally ratified, the rates will change to 17 SDRs per kilo of cargo and 1,000 SDRs per passenger for luggage. The franc's value is usually around 5½p.

The *bancor* was an international currency originally proposed by Keynes. Though the idea never materialised, it helped formulate SDRs. Prof R. Triffin had a similar idea to convert part of IMF funds into an international currency.

The term *international currency* is used to denote any currency or means of exchange which is generally accepted in the world. Dollars, sterling, yen, Swiss francs and the German mark are the main international currencies. Gold is no longer generally used as an international currency, except in settling some foreign debts. The international currency symbol is Ħ.

TAXES

2.1 Structure

The UK tax system has evolved over many centuries. Bits have been grafted on or amputated, not always cleanly, to meet particular needs or as a means of manipulating the economy in accordance with the wishes of the government of the day. Many provisions live on even though the circumstances they were designed to deal with have long since passed.

There are about forty taxes in the UK. The exact number depends on what you count as a tax and how you count the ones that you have decided are taxes.

Taxes are administered by two main government departments: Inland Revenue and HM Customs and Excise. These departments work independently and only exchange a limited amount of information.

The taxes administered by Inland Revenue are:

- Income tax
- Corporation tax
- Petroleum revenue tax
- Capital gains tax
- Inheritance tax
- Stamp duty
- Stamp duty reserve tax

The taxes administered by HM Customs and Excise are:

- Value-added tax
- Customs duties

[18]

- Excise duties
- Car tax

The Department of Social Security administers national insurance. The Department of Transport administers vehicles excise duty. Other government departments make certain charges which, it could be argued, are taxes (e.g. television licences). Local authorities administer the community charge (or 'poll tax').

2.2   Income tax

2.2.1   *Introduction*

Income tax was introduced in 1799 to pay for the war against Napoleon. It was a temporary tax and theoretically still is, requiring a new Act of Parliament each year. Even though we beat Napoleon in 1815, income tax has been levied every year since 1842.

Income tax is paid by individuals, partnerships and trusts (but not by companies or other associations). The tax is charged on income earned in the UK or earned overseas and remitted to the UK, and is determined by reference to the income tax year, which, for historical reasons, runs from 6 April to the following 5 April.

There are three steps to calculating a person's income tax:

1   calculate his income,
2   determine what deductions may be made,
3   apply tax rates to the difference.

The ramifications of these steps can become very complicated indeed, but we can provide a useful introduction as to how the system works.

2.2.2   *Income*

For income tax purposes, all sources of income are regarded as:

[19]

1 tax-free income,
2 earned income, or
3 investment income.

Between 1894 and 1984 investment income was taxed at a higher rate than was earned income. They are now taxed at the same rate, but it is still necessary to distinguish them for other tax purposes (such as loss relief).

Tax-free income comprises:

1 inherited money (subject to inheritance tax),
2 profit from non-commercial sales (subject to capital gains tax),
3 winnings from gambling,
4 scholarship, educational and housing grants,
5 social security payments, with the five exceptions given in section 2.2.3 below,
6 interest on national savings certificates,
7 the first £70 interest from a Post Office savings account,
8 golden handshakes (to a limit),
9 wedding presents and scholarship grants from an employer,
10 war widows' pensions, wound and disability pensions, payments from Germany or Austria to Nazi victims, payments for additional services in the armed forces, payments to holders of certain awards for gallantry,
11 maturity bonuses on Defence Bonds, British Savings Bonds, National Development Bonds and post-war credits,
12 the capital part of a life annuity and lump sum payment from a pension plan,
13 half of any profit-related pay,
14 adoption allowances under Children Act 1975,
15 interest on overpaid tax (repayment supplements),
16 awards made by a court,
17 bonuses at the end of a Save As You Earn contract,
18 receipts derived from an Act of Parliament or Royal Charter,
19 dividends received under a personal equity plan.

Earned income comprises:

1   all salaries, wages, fees, commissions, emoluments, stipends, honoraria, tips, etc.,
2   fringe benefits and perks which arise from your employment (such as company cars, cheap loans, free holidays, etc.), subject to many exceptions,
3   pensions and retirement annuities (but not the lump sum payments),
4   royalties if you created whatever gives rise to the income under a patent or copyright,
5   statutory sick pay, maternity pay and statutory maternity pay,
6   these social security payments:
    (a)   industrial death benefit,
    (b)   invalidity allowance (but not invalidity benefit),
    (c)   retirement pensions,
    (d)   unemployment benefit,
    (e)   widow's allowance, widowed mother's allowance and widow's pension (but not war pensions).

Investment income comprises:

1   rent (and similar payments from land),
2   dividends,
3   interest,
4   royalties, if you did not create whatever gives rise to the patent or copyright,
5   nominal value of owning woodlands.

2.2.3   Deductions

From your taxable income you may deduct the following:

1   personal allowances,
2   capital allowances,
3   reliefs,
4   annual payments,
5   expenses.

[21]

The main tax allowance is the personal allowance, which every taxpayer receives.

In 1806, it was decided that married women did not exist for tax purposes and that their income belonged to their husbands. While emancipation for women soon came in other areas, it was not until 1990 that women were emancipated for tax purposes.

From 1990, all women are regarded as taxpayers in their own right. Every married couple receives a married couple's tax allowance. This is given in the first instance to the husband, but may be transferred to his wife to the extent that he has insufficient income to use it.

There is also an additional personal allowance, claimable by a single parent or by a father with an incapacitated wife.

If a taxpayer is over 65, he or she is entitled to a higher personal allowance (age allowance). If, however, their income is above a set limit, the allowance is reduced by £1 for each £2 it exceeds that limit until it is down to the ordinary personal allowance. This allowance is increased again when the taxpayer reaches 75.

The married couple's allowance increases when either partner reaches 65, and again when either partner reaches 75. These higher married couple's allowances also reduce by any excess over the set limit until the ordinary married couple's allowance is reached.

A widow may claim the widow's bereavement allowance in the tax year of bereavement and the following year unless she remarries.

If you took out a qualifying life assurance policy before 14 March 1984, you are entitled to an allowance of 15 per cent of the premiums to a limit of one-sixth of your income.

There is an extra allowance for a taxpayer who is blind.

Capital allowances are a percentage of the expenditure on major items acquired for use in a business. The allowance is 4 per cent on a reducing balance basis for:

1   agricultural and forestry land and buildings,
2   dredging,
3   hotels,
4   industrial buildings and sports pavilions.

[22]

The allowance is 25 per cent on a reducing balance basis for:

1 know-how,
2 mines and oil wells,
3 motor cars (to a limit of £2,000 per year per car),
4 patent rights,
5 plant and machinery.

Scientific research attracts a 100 per cent initial allowance. Cemeteries and crematoria attract a special allowance.
The following reliefs are available:

1 *Loss relief.* A loss made by a business may be carried forward against future profits or, in certain circumstances, be carried back against income of previous years.
2 *Top-slicing relief.* Where an unusually large amount of income is received in one year, this relief allows it to be spread over 2 or more years in very limited circumstances.
3 *Double taxation relief.* If the same income is subject to tax in two countries, this relief usually restricts the total tax paid to that of the country with the higher tax rates.

Stock relief was abolished on 12 March 1984.
Annual payments are amounts which are regarded as the income of the recipient and are therefore deducted from the income of the person making the payment. The courts have held that many types of payment are annual payments, and more types could yet be decided. The commonest types are:

1 interest which is tax-deductible (such as mortage interest),
2 deeds of covenant and other settlements,
3 alimony and other payments arising from divorce,
4 50 per cent of class 4 national insurance contributions.

Expenses may be deducted only from the income to which they relate. If you are an employee, you can only deduct expenses which are wholly, exclusively and necessarily incurred in the performance of the duties of the employment. If you are self-employed, you do not have to show that the expense was necessary.

The more common deductible expenses are:

1 all costs and overheads of a business,
2 specific bad debts,
3 subscriptions to trade bodies and professional bodies,
4 travel in the course of work (but not to get to work),
5 entertaining staff (but no one else),
6 business gifts up to £10, with exceptions,
7 most interest payments,
8 pre-trading expenditure of the previous 5 years,
9 staff training and staff welfare,
10 theft of goods or takings,
11 most charitable donations.

Items not allowed as expenses include:

1 expenses of a personal rather than business nature,
2 drawings by a sole trader or partner,
3 depreciation (but a capital allowance may be claimable),
4 entertaining customers and suppliers,
5 political donations,
6 fines,
7 interest on late payment of tax,
8 losses covered by insurance,
9 unjustified contingent liabilities.

2.2.4 Rates of tax

Having calculated a person's taxable income and deducted everything permissible, you have the person's net taxable income. This is rounded down to the nearest whole pound.

The first chunk of income is taxed at a basic rate. Above this level, chunks of income are taxed at a higher rate. Currently there are just two rates: a basic rate of 25 per cent and a higher rate of 40 per cent.

The net taxable income multiplied by the rates of tax

[24]

gives you the figure for the tax borne. This is rounded down to the nearest penny. From this you deduct tax already paid (e.g. under the PAYE system, or deducted at source from dividends or interest payments) to give you the figure for tax payable.

2.3 Corporation tax

Corporation tax is paid by companies and other corporate bodies such as clubs and associations (though many clubs and associations will not be liable to tax at all). It was introduced in 1965, before which companies paid income tax and profits tax. Corporation tax still has many rules in common with income tax.

The income subject to corporation tax is the same as for income tax except that capital gains are included. (An individual pays capital gains tax instead.) For corporation tax purposes capital gains are referred to as 'chargeable gains'. Before 18 March 1987 chargeable gains assessable to tax were reduced by a fraction and the balance charged at the higher rate; chargeable gains are now taxed as for the rest of the company's profit.

A company cannot claim personal allowances (or any equivalent) or top-slicing relief. But there is an extra type of relief, namely group and consortium relief. A company within a group or consortium which makes a loss may offset some or all of that loss against profits earned elsewhere within the group or consortium. The rules regarding loss relief are different, though they follow the same principles.

Corporation tax is assessed not according to the income tax year but according to 'financial years'. These run from 1 April to the following 31 March, and are named from the calendar year in which they begin. Thus the 1988 financial year ran from 1 April 1988 to 31 March 1989.

The amount of the income is determined by taking the profits as per the accounts and adjusting them according to tax rules. You add items which have been deducted in the accounts but which are not tax-deductible (such as depreciation and political donations), and subtract items not

[25]

shown in the accounts but which are tax-deductible (such as capital allowances). The result is known as the 'adjusted profit'.

There are two rates of corporation tax: the higher rate and the lower rate. The higher rate is paid by companies with taxable profits above the upper limit, and the lower rate is paid by companies with taxable profits below the lower limit. Sometimes the two rates are called the large companies rate and the small companies rate. However, they have nothing to do with the size of the company, only the size of its adjusted profit.

When a company makes a dividend (or any other kind of distribution) it has to pay advance corporation tax (ACT). This is not (usually) an extra tax, as the amount of ACT is deducted from the company's corporation tax liability as calculated above. The balance is known as 'mainstream corporation tax' (MCT). ACT usually just brings forward the liability to pay some of the corporation tax.

The shareholder receiving a dividend is regarded as having received a larger amount on which he has already paid income tax. If he receives a dividend of £75, he is regarded as having received a dividend of £100 on which he has paid tax of £25 (the actual amount is shown on a certificate sent with the dividend). He must pay 25 per cent of that £100, i.e. £25, which he has already paid, meaning that he has no further liability for tax.

If, however, the shareholder is liable to pay tax at 40 per cent, he must pay over the extra £15 to the Revenue.

Broadly the same procedure applies to building society interest and dividends from unit trusts.

2.4 Capital gains tax

Capital gains tax (CGT) was introduced in 1965 to tax the profit made in a non-commercial sale. It would usually apply, for example, if you bought a picture or jewellery or shares and later sold them for a profit. CGT is an alternative to income tax; you cannot pay both taxes on the same profit.

The following items are not subject to capital gains tax:

1 your main residence,
2 wasting chattels (anything with a life of less than 50 years, including all animals and vehicles),
3 other chattels to a limit (£6,000 from 6 April 1989),
4 the disposal of a debt,
5 annuities and capital payments from a superannuation fund,
6 decorations for valour or gallantry,
7 foreign currency acquired for personal expenditure,
8 insurance policies,
9 savings certificates and non-marketable securities (this includes traditional options but not traded options); from 2 July 1986 it also applied to Government securities,
10 settlements (with some exceptions),
11 shares held under the Business Expansion Scheme;
12 qualifying corporate bonds.

A transfer is also exempt if it is:

1 to a newly incorporated business,
2 within a group of companies,
3 between husband and wife,
4 a gift for the public benefit,
5 of the nature of damages or compensation,
6 an agricultural grant,
7 within the scope of a Personal Equity Plan,
8 to do with a work of art (subject to rules),
9 on termination of a settlement,
10 a legacy,
11 a disposal of woodlands.

If an item does not fall within the scope of an exemption, it may still avoid tax by falling within the scope of one of these reliefs:

1 *Retirement relief.* The relief is £125,000 and half the balance up to £500,000. If you have owned the business or property for less than 10 years, the relief is proportionately limited.

2   *Roll-over relief.* This relief postpones a CGT charge if the proceeds of a sale are reinvested in a similar asset within 3 years. It applies to a curious ragbag of assets, namely, land and buildings, plant and machinery, ships, aircraft, hovercraft, spacecraft and satellites, goodwill, and EEC milk and potato quota payments.
3   *Hold-over relief.* This relief postpones a CGT charge when the disposal is other than 'at arm's length', e.g. a gift.

These reliefs are subject to detailed provisions regarding eligibility.

If a disposal is neither exempted nor relieved, the tax is charged on the loss of value to the original owner less:

1   increases which accrued before 6 April 1982,
2   indexation allowance, and
3   the annual exemption.

Indexation allowance seeks to stop CGT being a tax on inflation. Imagine you buy a painting for £10,000; 6 years later (during which there has been 40 per cent inflation) you sell it for £30,000. CGT is not charged on the whole £20,000 'profit', as part of that is simply inflation. You uprate the original price by the inflation (£10,000 + 40 per cent = £14,000) and charge CGT on the difference, namely £16,000. The retail price index is used as the measure of inflation, though in practice indices published by the Revenue are used.

There are special provisions for expenditure on property subject to a lease of less than 50 years, and for shares held from before March 1985.

The annual exemption is an amount which usually increases in the Budget each year. The current limit (1989–90) is £5,000. Trusts are usually entitled to only half this figure.

If exemptions, reliefs, indexation and the annual allowance still leave you with a taxable amount, it is added to your income and charged at the appropriate income tax rate.

[28]

2.5   Inheritance tax

Inheritance tax (IHT) is the name that was given to capital transfer tax (CTT) in 1984. CTT replaced estate duty in 1974. Estate duty was the last of the 'death duties' to be charged; the next to last, legacy duty, was abolished in 1947.

Inheritance tax is made on gifts which arise on the death of the donor or within 7 years of his death.

There is a band up to which no inheritance tax at all is payable. For 1989–90, this limit is £118,000. It is increased each year in line with inflation. The excess is taxed currently at 40 per cent.

For gifts made more than 3 years before death, the tax is reduced by these amounts:

Years before death	Tax reduced by (%)
0–3	nil
3–4	20
4–5	40
5–6	60
6–7	80
more than 7	100

The following gifts and inheritances are not subject to IHT:

1 gifts in consideration of marriage (to limits),
2 normal expenditure out of income,
3 dispositions to maintain one's family,
4 charitable donations,
5 political donations (limited to £100,000 on death or within 1 year of death),
6 transfers between husband and wife (limited to £55,000 if the husband or wife is not domiciled in the UK),
7 gifts to a specified museum,
8 gifts for the public benefit (subject to Treasury approval),
9 shares to an employee trust.

If someone dies within 5 years of inheriting, quick succession relief may be claimed. It is not necessary that the money or item inherited was still in the possession of the person who died. So if John inherits £10,000 and dies 2½ years later, he is entitled to 60 per cent quick succession relief. The value of John's estate for inheritance tax purposes is reduced by £6,000.

There are special rules regarding trusts.

2.6 Stamp duty

Stamp duty is one of the country's oldest taxes, dating from 1694. It is a curiosity in that it does not tax people, things or transactions, but the pieces of paper which give effect to transactions. If you can make a transaction without a piece of paper, you avoid the tax: so for goods sold against a bill of sale there is a charge to stamp duty, but if sold without a bill of sale, there is no stamp duty.

However, for many transactions, the law specifically states that the transaction must be in writing, so stamp duty cannot be avoided. The commonest examples are buying property and (until October 1991) buying shares.

Stamp duty is charged in one of two ways:

1   a fixed duty,
2   ad valorem duty.

Fixed duties used to be charged on common documents such as receipts and cheques, but they are now restricted to a much narrower range of documents. Fixed duties range from 50p to £2.

Ad valorem duty is based on the underlying value of the transaction, as follows:

1   Shares and marketable securities: 0.5 per cent.
2   Bearer certificates: 1.5 per cent.
3   Depositary receipts: 1.5 per cent.
4   Conveyance of property: 1 per cent (fixed duty if below £30,000).
5   Exchange or partition of a property: 1 per cent.
6   Formation of a company (capital duty): 1 per cent.

7   Insurance policies on life: assignment: 1 per cent (fixed duty if below £30,000).
8   Lease, consideration for: £1 per £100.
9   Lease: annual rental:
    up to 7 years: 50p per £500,
    7 to 35 years: £1 per £50,
    35 to 100 years: £6 per £50,
    over 100 years: £12 per £50.

The rates for consideration for a lease and the annual lease are actually determined by tables, which require the above calculations to be rounded up. A lease of less than 7 years at an annual rent of £500 or less attracts no ad valorem duty.

2.7   Stamp duty reserve tax

In contrast to stamp duty, this tax is the country's newest. It was born on 27 October 1986 to fill a gap left by the changes in stamp duty law on changes in the Stock Exchange on 'Big Bang' (27 October 1986). It charges a duty of 0.5 per cent on securities which are not subject to ad valorem stamp duty. Unlike stamp duty, it taxes transactions not documents. It is abolished from October 1991.

2.8   Value added tax

2.8.1   Introduction

Value added tax (VAT) was introduced in 1974 as a tax on most goods and services. Introducing it was a condition of Britain's joining the EEC. It replaced purchase tax (which applied only to selected goods) and selective employment tax.

VAT is charged on all goods and services unless they are specifically exempted or zero-rated. All other goods and services are standard-rated. The standard rate has been 15 per cent since 18 June 1979.

2.8.2   Operation

The tax works like this. A man buys goods for £20 and sells them for £30. He has generated 'value added' of £10, on which he pays value-added tax of 15 per cent, namely £1.50. He does this by paying £20 + 15 per cent (£23) when he buys the goods and collecting £30 + 15 per cent (£34.50) when he sells them. The difference of £11.50 comprises his £10 profit and £1.50 VAT. The £3 he paid to his supplier is called 'input tax', and the £4.50 he collected from his customer is 'output tax'. When he makes a VAT return (usually every 3 months), he simply totals his output tax and deducts his input tax from it.

If the goods are zero-rated, the trader charges no output tax but can claim back the input tax. If the goods are exempt, he charges no output tax but cannot claim back the input tax. The goods or service may be standard-rate, exempt or zero-rated when acquired, but taxed differently when supplied.

The effect of the different ratings can be shown if we assume that a trader has bought £20 worth of standard-rated goods on which he makes £10 profit. Depending on how the goods are classified when he sells them, the price will be:

	Standard-rated	Exempt	Zero-rated
Cost plus VAT	£23	£23	£23
Less input tax	£3	—	£3
	£20	£23	£20
Profit	£10	£10	£10
	£30	£33	£30
Output tax	£4.50	—	—
	£34.50	£33	£30

There are special provisions if you make a mixture of exempt supplies and taxed supplies (known as partial exemption). Traders who supply themselves with cars or stationery need to consider the self-supply rules. Retailers may use a special retail scheme (of which there are now twelve). Gifts, bad debts, theft, loss and errors all have special rules.

For supplies of the following second-hand items, VAT is only charged on the profit margin:

[32]

1   aircraft,
2   antiques, works of art and scientific collections,
3   boats and outboard motors,
4   caravans,
5   cars,
6   electronic organs,
7   firearms,
8   horses and ponies,
9   motorcycles.

2.8.3   *Zero-rated and exempt schedules*

These items are zero-rated:

1   food (not confectionery, catering, etc.),
2   sewage and water (except for industrial use),
3   books,
4   talking books for the blind,
5   news services,
6   fuel and power,
7   non-commercial construction,
8   work on protected buildings,
9   international services,
10 public transport, large ships and aircraft,
11 caravans and houseboats,
12 gold,
13 banknotes,
14 drugs, medicines and aid for the handicapped,
15 exports,
16 charities,
17 children's clothing, safety helmets, safety boots.

These items are exempt:

1   land,
2   insurance,
3   postal services,
4   betting, gaming and lotteries,
5   finance,
6   education,

7   health,
8   burial and cremation,
9   trade union fees and subscriptions to professional bodies,
10 sports competitions,
11 works of art.

The definition of what items fall within each item is discussed at great lengths in the 110 leaflets issued by VAT offices. Many times the distinctions become arbitrary: for example, dried banana chips are zero-rated as food, whereas dried pineapple pieces are standard-rated as confectionery!

It is obvious to see why food is zero-rated while confectionery is standard-rated, but these distinctions can lead to absurd results. For example, medicated lozenges are standard-rated while pork scratchings are zero-rated.

Despite the immense detail given in VAT leaflets, arguments still arise from time to time on how something should be classified. Recent arguments have included whether chewy cereal bars are food or confectionery, and whether scaly carp is zero-rated as food or standard-rated as fishing bait.

Perhaps you now understand the joke that VAT stands for Very Arbitrary Tax.

2.8.4   Registration

Unlike other taxes, you can only charge VAT if you are registered. You *must* register if your annual turnover is above a certain limit, and *may* register if it is below. (These provisions are subject to some exceptions.) The limit is changed every year in the Budget. For 1990–91 the limit is £25,400.

If your turnover falls below £24,400 you can apply to be deregistered.

On registration you are given a VAT number in the form NNN NNNN NN. The validity of a VAT number can be checked by the 'rule of 97'. You multiply each of the first seven numbers by 8, 7, 6, 5, 4, 3 and 2 respectively and add the last two-digit number. The result should be exactly divisible by 97.

Thus to check 479 9776 50:

$$
\begin{aligned}
4 \times 8 &= 32 \\
7 \times 7 &= 49 \\
9 \times 6 &= 54 \\
9 \times 5 &= 45 \\
7 \times 4 &= 28 \\
7 \times 3 &= 21 \\
6 \times 2 &= \underline{12} \\
& 241 \\
+ \ & \underline{50} \\
& 291
\end{aligned}
$$

As $291 = 97 \times 3$, the VAT number is valid.

2.9 Car tax

This is a vestige of the old purchase tax which was otherwise abolished in 1974. The car tax charges 10 per cent sales tax on a new car and 6 per cent on a new caravan.

It should be distinguished from vehicle excise duty (or road tax), which is an annual charge made by the Department of Transport, evidenced by a tax disc displayed in the car.

2.10 Customs duties

Customs duties are part of the general control of imports and exports from the country. These controls also aim to enforce the laws on smuggling, contraband, drugs, pornography and protected species. Some form of Customs duties has existed since 1055. Duties on imports faded out in the eighteenth century. The system was extensively revised from 1 January 1988 under a programme known as Customs 88.

Under the new scheme one document (the Single Administrative Document, or SAD) is used for both the

[35]

export and import documents. This document is now accepted by most countries of the world.

Each product must be classified according to a Tariff Coding, which can be up to eleven digits long. The duty payable and the exact procedure to be followed are governed by voluminous instructions published by Customs and Excise.

2.11   Excise duties

Excise duties charge a tax on certain ranges of goods. In the seventeenth and eighteenth centuries, excise duties were the major revenue earner for the government. They have slowly disappeared and are now charged on just five categories:

1   hydrocarbon oil,
2   tobacco products,
3   alcoholic liquor,
4   betting and gaming,
5   matches and mechanical lighters.

2.12   National insurance

Strictly speaking national insurance is not a tax at all but a compulsory insurance policy. However, it bears more relation to a tax than to insurance and is more conveniently considered as such.

National insurance is levied under four classes:

Class 1 is paid in respect of employees. Part is paid by the employee (primary contribution) and part by the employer (secondary contribution).
Class 2 is a fixed weekly amount paid by the self-employed.
Class 3 is a voluntary contribution.
Class 4 is a figure, calculated as a percentage between an upper and lower limit, payable by the self-employed.

The employee pays no national insurance to a lower earnings limit. Above this he pays NI on all his wages (not

[36]

just the excess) until the upper earnings limit is reached. The employer only pays NI for employees who earn above the lower earnings limit, but there is no upper limit for the employer. For low earnings above the lower limit, reduced rates apply for both the employer and employee. A married woman who made an election before 11 May 1977 to pay a reduced rate can continue doing so, but no new elections can be made. If the company runs an adequate pension scheme, the *company* may contract out its employees. The employer and employee then pay class 1 NI at a contracted-out rate.

An employee may now contract himself out of the state pension scheme. He still pays the full rate of national insurance, but part of it is refunded to his pension scheme.

Although national insurance is generally administered by the Department of Social Security (DSS), class 4 is administered entirely by the Inland Revenue, and class 1 is collected by the Inland Revenue (under the PAYE scheme).

The eligibility for some social security benefits depends on reaching a qualifying factor according to the number and amounts of class 1, 2 and 3 (never class 4) contributions paid. This is determined by reference to incredibly complicated rules. If you fail to meet your earnings factor, you make voluntary class 3 contributions to top it up.

ECONOMIC MEASURES

3.1 Retail price index

The commonest measure of inflation is the Retail Price Index (RPI). This takes a selection of items as would be spent by the average family and measures by how much their prices have risen or fallen each month.

In January 1987, the RPI was rebased. This means that other indices are expressed as a ratio to the January 1987 index of 100.0. So the September 1989 index of 117.50 means that items which, on average, cost £100 in January 1987 cost £117.50 in September 1989.

The index only refers to increases in retail prices. With the curious exception of mortgage repayments, it does not include any costs of borrowing money. The index is therefore unaffected by increases or decreases in interest rates. However if currency fluctuations change the price of imported goods, or if VAT changes affect the price of supplies, these will affect the index.

An index is part of a fraction. To measure the increased cost of, say, £500 worth of goods from June 1980 to October 1989, you use the indices for those months to make the fraction 117.5/67.4 by which you multiply £500. This gives you £871.66, and means that £500 worth of retail goods in June 1980 would, on average, cost you £871.66 in October 1989.

A full index is given in Table 3.1. Figures before January 1987 have been calculated by the author.

TABLE 3.1 Retail price index (1987 basis)

Year	Jan.	Feb.	Mar.	Apr.	May	June	July	Aug.	Sep.	Oct.	Nov.	Dec.
1947	—	—	—	—	—	7.3	7.3	7.3	7.4	7.4	7.6	7.6
1948	7.6	7.8	7.8	7.9	7.9	8.1	7.9	7.9	7.9	7.9	8.0	8.0
1949	8.0	8.0	8.0	8.0	8.1	8.1	8.1	8.1	8.2	8.2	8.2	8.3
1950	8.3	8.3	8.3	8.4	8.4	8.4	8.4	8.3	8.4	8.4	8.5	8.5
1951	8.6	8.6	8.6	8.9	9.1	9.2	9.2	9.3	9.4	9.5	9.5	9.5
1952	9.7	9.8	9.8	9.9	9.9	10.1	10.1	10.0	10.0	10.1	10.1	10.1
1953	10.1	10.2	10.3	10.3	10.3	10.3	10.3	10.3	10.3	10.3	10.3	10.3
1954	10.3	10.3	10.3	10.4	10.3	10.4	10.6	10.6	10.5	10.6	10.6	10.6
1955	10.7	10.7	10.7	10.8	10.8	11.0	11.0	10.9	11.0	11.2	11.3	11.3
1956	11.3	11.3	11.4	11.6	11.5	11.5	11.5	11.5	11.5	11.6	11.6	11.6
1957	11.7	11.7	11.7	11.8	11.8	11.9	12.0	12.0	12.0	12.0	12.1	12.2
1958	12.2	12.1	12.2	12.3	12.3	12.4	12.2	12.2	12.2	12.3	12.3	12.4
1959	12.4	12.4	12.4	12.3	12.3	12.3	12.4	12.3	12.2	12.3	12.4	12.4
1960	12.3	12.3	12.3	12.4	12.4	12.5	12.5	12.4	12.4	12.5	12.6	12.6
1961	12.6	12.6	12.7	12.8	12.8	12.9	12.9	13.0	13.0	13.0	13.2	13.2
1962	13.2	13.2	13.3	13.5	13.5	13.6	13.5	13.4	13.4	13.4	13.4	13.5
1963	13.6	13.7	13.7	13.7	13.7	13.7	13.7	13.6	13.7	13.7	13.7	13.8
1964	13.8	13.8	13.9	14.0	14.1	14.2	14.2	14.2	14.2	14.3	14.4	14.4
1965	14.5	14.5	14.5	14.8	14.9	14.9	14.9	14.9	14.9	15.0	15.0	15.1
1966	15.1	15.1	15.1	15.3	15.4	15.5	15.4	15.5	15.5	15.5	15.6	15.6
1967	15.7	15.7	15.7	15.8	15.8	15.8	15.7	15.8	15.8	15.8	15.9	16.0
1968	16.1	16.1	16.2	16.2	16.5	16.5	16.6	16.6	16.6	16.8	16.8	17.0
1969	17.1	17.2	17.2	17.4	17.4	17.5	17.5	17.4	17.5	17.6	17.6	17.8
1970	17.9	18.0	18.1	18.4	18.4	18.5	18.6	18.6	18.7	18.9	19.0	19.2
1971	19.4	19.5	19.7	20.1	20.3	20.4	20.5	20.5	20.5	20.7	20.8	20.9
1972	21.0	21.1	21.2	21.4	21.5	21.6	21.7	21.9	22.0	22.3	22.4	22.5
1973	22.6	22.8	22.0	23.4	23.5	23.7	23.8	23.8	24.0	24.5	24.7	24.9
1974	25.4	25.8	26.0	26.9	27.3	27.6	27.8	27.8	28.1	28.7	29.2	29.6
1975	30.4	30.9	31.5	32.7	34.1	34.8	35.1	35.3	35.6	36.1	36.6	37.0
1976	37.5	38.0	38.2	38.9	39.4	39.6	39.6	40.2	40.7	41.5	42.0	42.6
1977	43.7	44.1	44.6	45.7	46.1	46.6	46.6	46.8	47.1	47.3	47.5	47.8
1978	48.0	48.3	48.6	49.3	49.6	50.0	50.3	50.6	50.8	51.0	51.3	51.8
1979	52.5	53.0	54.0	54.3	54.7	55.7	58.1	58.5	59.1	59.7	60.3	60.7
1980	62.2	63.1	63.9	66.1	66.7	67.4	68.0	68.1	68.5	68.9	69.5	69.9
1981	70.3	70.9	72.0	74.1	74.6	75.0	75.3	75.9	76.3	77.0	77.8	78.3
1982	78.8	78.8	79.5	81.1	81.6	81.9	81.9	81.9	81.9	82.3	82.7	82.5
1983	82.6	83.0	83.1	84.3	84.7	84.9	85.3	85.7	86.1	86.4	86.7	86.9
1984	86.9	87.2	87.5	88.7	89.0	89.2	89.1	90.0	90.1	90.7	91.0	91.0
1985	91.3	92.0	92.8	94.8	95.2	95.4	95.3	95.5	95.5	95.6	95.9	96.1
1986	96.3	96.6	96.8	97.7	97.9	97.8	97.5	97.8	98.3	98.5	99.3	99.6
1987	100.0	100.4	100.6	101.8	101.9	101.9	101.8	102.1	102.4	102.9	103.4	103.3
1988	103.3	103.7	104.1	105.8	106.2	106.6	106.7	107.9	108.4	109.5	110.0	110.3
1989	111.0	111.9	112.4	114.4	115.1	115.6	115.5	115.8	116.6	117.5	118.5	118.8
1990	119.5	120.2	121.4	125.1	126.2	126.7	126.8	128.1	129.3			

3.2 Rate of inflation

The rate of inflation is the amount by which the retail price index increases from one year to the next. This is given as a percentage. See Table 3.2.

[39]

TABLE 3.2   Rates of inflation

Year	Jan.	Feb.	Mar.	Apr.	May	June	July	Aug.	Sep.	Oct.	Nov.	Dec.
1948	—	—	—	—	—	9.7	7.2	7.9	7.6	7.0	5.1	4.9
1949	4.6	2.9	2.3	0.6	2.6	1.3	3.0	3.1	3.2	3.6	3.3	3.5
1950	3.6	3.7	4.2	4.9	3.3	2.3	2.2	1.7	2.0	2.5	2.9	3.2
1951	3.9	4.6	5.0	6.3	8.7	9.6	11.3	12.2	12.3	11.9	11.9	12.0
1952	13.0	12.0	11.8	11.8	9.1	10.6	8.8	7.6	6.7	6.9	6.3	6.4
1953	4.4	4.6	4.8	4.1	3.8	2.5	2.7	2.6	2.6	1.7	2.2	1.0
1954	1.4	0.9	1.1	0.6	0.6	0.7	2.4	2.4	2.4	2.8	3.0	4.0
1955	4.1	4.4	3.4	3.5	3.6	5.2	3.8	3.8	4.6	5.3	6.4	5.8
1956	5.1	5.1	6.4	7.3	7.3	5.0	4.3	5.2	4.4	3.9	2.7	3.0
1957	4.4	4.3	2.8	1.8	2.0	3.2	4.5	4.0	3.9	4.3	4.5	4.6
1958	3.5	3.2	4.1	4.9	4.4	4.3	1.8	1.8	2.2	2.1	1.9	1.8
1959	2.1	2.5	1.8	−0.1	−0.1	−0.8	0.5	0.9	0.3	−0.2	0.2	0.0
1960	−0.5	−0.4	−0.5	0.7	1.1	1.5	1.9	1.0	1.7	2.0	1.7	1.8
1961	2.2	2.2	2.7	2.7	3.0	3.3	3.2	4.8	4.5	3.9	4.5	4.4
1962	4.6	4.7	4.8	5.6	5.7	5.5	5.1	3.2	3.3	2.9	2.3	2.6
1963	2.7	3.5	3.2	2.1	1.7	1.0	0.8	1.4	1.8	2.3	2.2	1.9
1964	2.0	1.2	1.5	2.0	3.0	3.4	4.0	4.7	4.4	4.1	4.6	4.8
1965	4.6	4.5	4.5	5.6	5.1	4.9	4.9	4.7	4.8	4.8	4.4	4.5
1966	4.4	4.5	4.3	3.6	3.9	3.9	3.5	3.9	3.6	3.8	4.0	3.7
1967	3.7	3.7	3.5	3.0	2.2	2.4	2.2	1.4	1.5	2.0	2.0	2.5
1968	2.6	3.0	3.4	4.4	4.6	4.6	5.3	5.7	5.9	5.6	5.2	5.9
1969	5.4	6.2	6.2	6.3	5.5	5.3	5.3	4.9	5.1	5.4	5.4	4.7
1970	5.0	4.9	5.1	5.6	6.1	5.9	6.7	6.8	7.0	7.4	7.9	7.9
1971	8.5	8.5	8.8	9.4	9.8	10.3	10.2	10.3	9.9	9.4	9.2	9.0
1972	8.2	8.1	7.6	6.3	6.1	6.1	5.8	6.6	7.0	7.9	7.6	7.7
1973	7.7	7.9	8.2	9.2	9.5	9.3	9.4	8.9	9.3	9.9	10.3	10.6
1974	12.0	13.2	13.5	15.2	16.0	16.5	17.1	16.9	17.1	17.1	18.3	19.1
1975	19.9	19.9	21.2	21.7	25.0	26.1	26.3	26.9	26.6	25.9	25.2	24.9
1976	23.4	22.9	21.2	18.9	15.4	13.8	12.9	13.8	14.3	14.7	15.0	15.1
1977	16.6	16.2	16.7	17.5	17.1	17.7	17.6	16.5	15.6	14.1	13.0	12.1
1978	9.9	9.5	9.1	7.9	7.7	7.4	7.8	8.0	7.8	7.8	8.1	8.4
1979	9.3	9.6	9.8	10.1	10.3	11.4	15.6	15.8	16.5	17.2	17.4	17.2
1980	18.4	19.1	19.8	21.8	21.9	21.0	16.9	16.3	15.9	15.4	15.3	15.1
1981	13.0	12.5	12.6	12.0	11.7	11.3	10.9	11.5	11.4	11.7	12.0	12.0
1982	12.0	11.0	10.4	9.4	9.5	9.2	8.7	8.0	7.3	6.8	6.3	5.4
1983	4.9	5.3	4.6	4.0	3.7	3.7	4.2	4.6	5.1	5.0	4.8	5.3
1984	5.1	5.1	5.2	5.2	5.1	5.1	4.5	5.0	4.7	5.9	4.9	4.6
1985	5.0	5.4	6.1	6.9	7.0	7.0	6.9	6.2	5.9	5.4	5.5	5.7
1986	5.5	5.1	4.2	3.0	2.8	2.5	2.4	2.4	3.0	3.0	3.5	3.7
1987	3.9	3.9	4.0	4.2	4.1	4.2	4.4	4.4	4.2	4.5	4.1	3.7
1988	3.3	3.3	3.5	3.9	4.2	4.6	4.8	5.7	5.9	6.4	6.4	6.8
1989	7.5	7.8	7.9	8.0	8.3	8.3	8.2	7.3	7.6	7.3	7.7	7.7
1990	7.7	7.5	8.1	9.4	9.7	9.8	9.8	10.6	10.9			

3.3   Purchasing power of the pound

Another way of looking at the effect of inflation is to consider how much £1 now is worth compared with £1 at the turn of the century. See Table 3.3.

TABLE 3.3   Inflation, 1900–89

Year	1900 = 100p	Year	1900 = 100p
1900	100p	1946	35.0p
1901	100p	1947	32.8p
1902	100p	1948	30.5p
1903	100p	1949	29.8p
1904	100p	1950	28.9p
1905	100p	1951	26.5p
1906	100p	1952	25.0p
1907	95.4p	1953	24.6p
1908	95.4p	1954	24.2p
1909	95.4p	1955	23.4p
1910	95.4p	1956	22.4p
1911	92.8p	1957	21.7p
1912	92.8p	1958	21.1p
1913	92.8p	1959	21.0p
1914	92.8p	1960	20.8p
1915	75.2p	1961	20.2p
1916	63.6p	1962	19.4p
1917	52.6p	1963	19.1p
1918	45.6p	1964	18.5p
1919	43.1p	1965	17.6p
1920	37.2p	1966	17.0p
1921	41.0p	1967	16.5p
1922	50.5p	1968	15.8p
1923	53.1p	1969	15.0p
1924	52.8p	1970	14.1p
1925	52.6p	1971	12.9p
1926	53.9p	1972	12.0p
1927	55.1p	1973	11.0p
1928	55.7p	1974	9.5p
1929	56.6p	1975	7.6p
1930	58.6p	1976	6.6p
1931	62.8p	1977	5.7p
1932	64.4p	1978	5.3p
1933	66.0p	1979	4.6p
1934	65.6p	1980	3.7p
1935	64.8p	1981	3.5p
1936	62.8p	1982	3.2p
1937	59.9p	1983	3.1p
1938	59.2p	1984	2.9p

TABLE 3.3   Inflation, 1900–89 – *cont*

Year	1900 = 100p	Year	1900 = 100p
1985	2.7p	1988	2.3p
1986	2.5p	1989	2.1p
1987	2.4p		

3.4   *Financial Times* indices

One measure of the economy is reflected in the share prices of companies quoted on the Stock Exchange. Further details on shares are given in chapter 13, but here we are concerned with their use as a measure of the economy.

A company may issue a share for 100p. That usually means that when a company first starts trading its shareholders pay 100p for each share they buy. If 100 shareholders each buy 1000 shares at 100p, the company has a share capital of £100,000, of which each shareholder owns 1 per cent. As the company establishes its reputation, earns profits and acquires assets, it becomes more valuable. The company may become worth, say, £163,000. As each shareholder still owns 1 per cent of the company, each share will now be worth 163p.

For quoted companies, share prices are affected by two sets of factors which may be broadly distinguished as:

1   those which affect the whole economy, and
2   those which affect just the company or its trade.

These are measured by what are known as the alpha coefficient and the beta factor respectively. (These terms have no connection with 'alpha shares' and 'beta shares'.) This leads us into a complex area of financial analysis, or at least would do if I weren't about to change the subject! Suffice it to say that the alpha coefficient is usually much more relevant than the beta factor.

As share prices largely reflect the perception of how investors see the economy as a whole, the alpha coefficient is a useful measure. Note that this reflects how the economy is perceived to be performing, not necessarily how it actually is performing.

The problem is how to strip out the beta factors. If a share price rises from 120p to 150p, it is a fact that it has risen by 30p or 25 per cent. But to say that 10p of this was due to the company and 20p to the economy is a subjective opinion. So instead a yardstick is produced by averaging a range of companies. This yardstick is the *Financial Times* index. Note that it does not strip out the beta factors, it just averages them out. The index takes the form of a single number.

The *Financial Times* actually produces hundreds of indices every day. However, the commonest are the FT Ordinary Share Index and the *Financial Times*–Stock Exchange 100 index.

The Ordinary Share index started in 1935 and is the oldest. It takes only 30 of the 7,000 or so shares quoted, converts them to a comparable base and takes the geometric mean. The geometric mean is calculated by multiplying the 30 prices and taking the thirtieth root. For an average (or arithmetic mean) you would multiply the prices and divide by 30.

A geometric mean is used in preference to the arithmetic mean to indicate the pattern of share price movements. Suppose we had just two shares worth 100p in our index and one doubled in value and the other halved. A geometric mean, the square root of 200 × 50, would still be 100, indicating that there had been no movement in the shares. An arithmetic mean (200 + 50) ÷ 2 would give us 125, implying that there had been an overall increase in share prices of 25 per cent.

Recently the 100 share index has become more popular. It draws on 100 companies instead of just 30 and is calculated more frequently. It is usually indicated 'FT-SE 100', which has lead to its nickname of 'Footsie'. It was introduced in February 1984. Like the 30-share index it is calculated as a geometric mean.

The *Financial Times* also publishes a series of '*Financial Times*-Actuaries Share Indices'. These give the same information but according to particular trades or areas of business. Indices are also published for collections (or 'equity groups') of business. These are themselves collected as the 'All-Share Index', drawing on about 730 companies. These indices were started in April 1962.

On 21 March 1987, the newspaper also launched the FT-Actuaries World Indices. This draws on 2,400 share prices from 23 countries. The base of 100 applies to 31 December 1986. Unlike the other FT indices, it uses arithmetic means. On 29 October 1990, the FT introduced a European index.

The newspaper also publishes indices for government securities, fixed interest deposits and shares in gold mines, plus indices for overseas countries (particularly the Dow-Jones for the US and the Nikkei-Dow Index for Japan), options, futures, unit trusts and commodities, as well as figures of Stock Exchange activity.

3.5 Banking base rates

A method which has increasingly been used to regulate the economy is the banking base rate. This is the rate which in practice is used for setting all other interest rates. For example, if you borrow money from the bank, you will be quoted a rate like 'base rate plus 3 per cent'. So if the base rate is 9 per cent, you will pay interest of 12 per cent. Your interest rate will go up and down with the base rate.

Up to 1971 the Bank of England set the base rate. In 1971 this was replaced by the Minimum Lending Rate (MLR), which up to 1978 was fixed by reference to the average rate quoted on Treasury bills. Since then it has been fixed by administrative decision.

In 1981, the individual banks were free to set their own rates. However in practice they follow each other closely.

Rates for recent years are given in Table 3.4.

3.6 Money supply

An obvious economic measure is simply the amount of money collectively owned by everyone in the country. The problem is how to define 'money'. In practice different definitions have been developed thus (see p. 46):

Economic Measures

TABLE 3.4   Base rates

From	Rate (%)	From	Rate (%)
1 November 1978	10	23 November 1984	9½
9 November 1978	12½	11 January 1985	10½
8 February 1979	14	14 January 1985	12
1 March 1979	13	28 January 1985	14
5 April 1979	12	20 March 1985	13½
15 June 1979	14	3 April 1985	13¼
19 November 1979	17	12 April 1985	12¾
4 July 1980	16	12 June 1985	12½
25 November 1980	14	15 July 1985	12
12 March 1981	12	29 July 1985	11½
16 September 1981	14	9 January 1986	12½
1 October 1981	16	19 March 1986	11½
14 October 1981	15½	9 April 1986	11
10 November 1981	15	21 April 1986	10½
4 December 1981	14½	27 May 1986	10
25 January 1982	14	15 October 1986	11
25 February 1982	13½	10 March 1987	10½
12 March 1982	13	18 March 1987	10
8 June 1982	12½	28 April 1987	9½
14 July 1982	12	11 May 1987	9
2 August 1982	11½	7 August 1987	10
18 August 1982	11	26 October 1987	9½
31 August 1982	10½	5 November 1987	9
7 October 1982	10	4 December 1987	8½
14 October 1982	9½	1 February 1988	9
5 November 1982	9	18 March 1988	8½
29 November 1982	10¼	8 April 1988	8
12 January 1983	11	17 May 1988	7½
15 March 1983	10½	3 June 1988	8
15 April 1983	10	6 June 1988	8½
15 June 1983	9½	22 June 1988	9
4 October 1983	9	28 June 1988	9½
15 March 1984	8½	4 July 1988	10
10 May 1984	9¼	18 July 1988	10½
9 July 1984	10	8 August 1988	11
12 July 1984	12	25 August 1988	12
9 August 1984	11½	25 November 1988	13
10 August 1984	11	24 May 1989	14
20 August 1984	10½	5 October 1989	15
7 November 1984	10	8 October 1990	14

M0 = notes and coins only,
M1 = M0 + current accounts,
M2 = M1 + deposit accounts,
M3 = M2 + other deposits,
M4 = M3 + building society accounts,
M5 = M4 adjusted for private holdings of certain money
market instruments.

To be more precise, M1 includes chequeable sterling current accounts. M2 adds sterling deposit accounts of private sector UK residents with the deposit bank and similar deposits with the discount houses. M3 adds sterling deposit accounts held by private sector UK residents with other banks, all non-sterling deposits of the private sector, and all deposits of the public sector. Before 1976, M3 also included foreign currency deposits of UK residents. M4 and M5 are recent inventions.

Of these classifications, M2 is no longer quoted in official bulletins. M1 is sometimes called 'narrow money' and M3 is sometimes called 'broad money'. M3 excluding UK private sector deposits in other currencies is given separately as 'sterling M3' or '£M3'. Figures for M3 money supply were effectively discontinued after summer 1989. Only M0, M4 and M5 are generally quoted now.

Figures quoted for the money supply are usually seasonally adjusted.

3.7 Balance of payments

Except to the extent that a nation is self-sufficient, it has to trade with other countries. The figures for balance of payments are effectively the income and expenditure account for the country.

Trade in tangible goods (cars, food etc) is referred to as 'visible trade'. Trade in such things as insurance and financial services is referred to as 'invisible trade'.

Recent figures for the balance of payments are given in Table 3.5

TABLE 3.5   Balance of payments (£m)

	1975	1976	1977	1978	1979	1980	1981	1982	1983	1984	1985	1986	1987	1988
Visible														
export	19,330	23,191	31,728	35,063	40,687	47,422	50,977	55,565	60,776	70,367	77,988	72,656	79,421	80,602
import	22,663	29,120	34,012	36,605	44,136	46,061	47,617	53,234	61,611	74,751	81,120	82,020	90,350	101,428
balance	−3,333	−3,929	−2,284	−1,542	−2,449	+1,361	+3,360	+2,331	−835	−4,384	−3,112	−9,364	−10,929	−20,826
Invisible														
balance	+1,751	+3,009	+2,148	+2,507	+2,732	+1,568	+2,799	+1,606	+3,969	+5,596	+6,335	+9,430	+7,258	+6,209
Overall														
balance	−1,582	−920	−136	+965	−717	+2,929	+6,159	+3,937	+3,134	+1,212	+3,223	+66	−3,671	−14,617

Source: Central Statistical Office.

[47]

3.8 Public spending

Just as the balance of payments effectively shows how the country as a whole trades with the rest of the world, so public spending figures show how the government 'trades' with its citizens.

Government income is derived mostly from taxation. Some comes from government shares in public corporations (those that make a profit). Recently the state coffers have been swollen with the proceeds of privatisation issues.

Expenditure is allocated on departmental budgets. Within departments, sums are 'voted' to particular projects or functions. Other government sums are handed over to other bodies to spend, such as the National Health Service and local authorities. Some money is allocated to a 'reserve' – a piggy bank for additional needs not separately budgeted for.

The main statement for public spending is made in the autumn as a white paper. Details of how the funds are to be raised are announced in the Budget, which is now usually introduced in March.

Traditionally the government spends more than it 'earns'. The difference is known as the Public Sector Borrowing Requirement (PSBR) and is funded by gilt-edged stock.

Since 1988, there has been an excess of receipts over expenditure. This has been named the Public Sector Debt Repayment (PSDR), which is being used to reduce the historic national debt.

A summary of public sector spending and proposed spending is given in Table 3.6.

3.9 Gross domestic product and gross national product

Two common measures of the economy are Gross Domestic Product (GDP) and Gross National Product (GNP).

GDP measures the total output of goods and services over a specific period (usually 1 year). It aggregates the

TABLE 3.6   Public spending (£m)

	1987–8 outturn	1988–9 outturn	1989–90 estimate	1990–1 plan	1991–2 plan
Central government expenditure	111,188	116,330	126,500	137,800	145,300
Support to local authorities	35,654	36,450	38,100	41,800	43,800
Finance for public corporations	793	−183	1,540	1,390	2,310
Privatisation proceeds	−5,140	−7,065	−4,250	−5,000	−5,000
Adjustments	—	—	−200	—	—
Planning total	142,495	145,532	161,700	179,000	192,300
Total public expenditure	172,523	178,594	196,300	210,400	222,200

Source: The Autumn Statement 1989 (HMSO).

amount expended on *final* goods and services, (i.e. omitting intermediate stages). GNP comprises the GDP plus income accruing to UK residents from overseas investment less income earned in the UK by foreign investors.

These measures of GDP and GNP ignore taxes and subsidies. They are therefore sometimes referred to as 'gross domestic product at market prices', or, colloquially, as 'money GDP'.

The GDP can also be stated at 'factor cost', which is the value representing only the sum of the units of the income's of the factors of production. In other words, it is the GDP at market prices less indirect taxes plus subsidies.

To this can be added net property income from abroad, while capital consumption is subtracted. The result is known as 'net national product at factor cost', or, more simply, 'national income'. This is the measure of the money value of the goods and services becoming available to the nation from economic activity.

Gross National Product is basically the GDP plus net income from abroad, and is usually stated at 1985 market prices. These prices can be adjusted to 'factor cost', as for GDP.

It should be remembered that there are many other similar economic measures in the CSO 'Blue Book'.

The figures for money GDP, national income (GDP), and GNP at 1985 factor cost (i.e. GNP national income plus capital consumption) are given in Table 3.7. These statistics are also published adjusted for inflation, and in the form of indices.

[49]

TABLE 3.7   Recent GDP and GNP figures (£m)

	1975	1976	1977	1978	1979	1980	1981
Money GDP	105,718	124,982	145,699	168,123	197,831	231,272	254,293
Nat. income	84,273	99,854	113,015	130,570	151,182	172,361	187,766
GNP (factor)	256,776	264,468	268,204	277,112	285,259	277,166	275,887
	1982	1983	1984	1985	1986	1987	1988
Money GDP	278,406	303,632	324,440	355,329	380,623	417,778	463,933
Nat. income	205,546	227,106	245,107	266,736	284,217	312,176	345,637
GNP (factor)	280,937	292,471	298,972	308,622	321,208	334,889	349,846

Source: Central Statistical Office.

3.10   Exchange rates

Up to 1971, the rates at which the currencies of the world could be exchanged were generally fixed. The Bretton Woods agreement of 1944 fixed currencies to a set rate relative to the US dollar. Currencies were allowed to float only within 1 per cent of that rate. The US itself secured its currency against gold by being committed to buy gold on demand at a fixed rate ($35.0875 per oz).

In 1971 this arrangement was dismantled, though various replacement schemes were briefly tried in the process. Since June 1972 sterling (and most other world currencies) have 'floated', that is there is no fixed exchange rate. Currencies move according to supply and demand. The currencies are not, however, entirely hostage to such international market forces, as each nation can draw on its gold and foreign exchange reserves to 'prop up' or force down its exchange rate.

A nation's exchange rate can therefore be seen to a limited extent as the nation's 'share price' expressed in another currency. However, pragmatic considerations interfere in this process. As the pound becomes worth more in foreign currency, our exports become more expensive and competing imports become cheaper. Therefore there is the desire for economic management to depress a currency's value, leading to the paradox that the British economy has been considerably stronger since the value of £1 fell below $2.

Up to 1949 the UK exchange rate was £1 = $4.03 (hence the colloquial use of the word 'dollar' for five shillings, 25p). In September 1949 the pound was devalued to $2.80; in November 1967 it was further devalued to $2.40. Since sterling floated freely, the general drift has been downwards. Recent annual average rates for which £1 could be converted to one of the other major currencies are given in Table 3.8 overleaf.

3.11   Sterling index

Any given exchange rate is a factor of two separate and (usually) independent economies. One pound may buy more US currency because of events in either country.

To give an idea of how UK currency is doing on its own, an approximation is made by the sterling index. This compares the exchange rate of the pound against a selection of other currencies in the ratio in which the UK trades with those countries. The result is expressed as a single number, using January 1975 as the base of 100.

Recent annual averages are:

1975	100.0	1980	96.1	1985	78.3
1976	85.7	1981	95.3	1986	72.8
1977	81.2	1982	90.7	1987	72.6
1978	81.5	1983	83.3	1988	75.5 (to Sep.)
1979	87.3	1984	78.8		

3.12   Gold

Gold is number 79 in the list of the 92 naturally occurring chemical elements. It is the most malleable and ductile of all elements; it can be beaten so thin that it is possible to see through it. Its few practical uses include electrical contacts and as a reflective shield in some aircraft cockpit windows. Gold reacts with few chemicals but easily forms alloys with other metals.

As an alloy its purity is traditionally measured in 'carats', where each carat represents $1/24$ of the alloy's mix; thus 18 carat gold is $18/24$ gold, i.e. $3/4$ gold and $1/4$ base metal. Also

[51]

TABLE 3.8 Exchange rates

	1975	1976	1977	1978	1979	1980	1981	1982	1983	1984	1985	1986	1987	1988*
US dollar	2.220	1.805	1.745	1.920	2.123	2.328	2.025	1.749	1.516	1.336	1.298	1.467	1.639	1.683
French franc	9.50	8.61	8.57	8.64	9.03	9.83	10.94	11.48	11.55	11.63	11.55	10.16	9.84	10.69
German d-mark	5.447	4.552	4.050	3.851	3.887	4.227	4.556	4.243	3.870	3.791	3.784	3.183	2.941	3.143
Italian lira	1,447	1,497	1,540	1,628	1,762	1,992	2,287	2,364	2,302	2,339	2,463	2,186	2,123	2,344
Japanese yen	658.1	535.4	467.7	402.7	465.5	525.6	444.6	435.2	359.9	316.8	307.1	246.8	236.5	226.3
Swiss franc	5.723	4.521	4.189	3.423	3.527	3.894	3.969	3.547	3.182	3.130	3.155	2.635	2.439	2.654

*The figure for 1988 only covers the year to September.

Source: Central Statistical Office.

[52]

traditionally, gold is weighed by means of Troy weight. A Troy ounce is 31.1035 grams (the standard ounce is 28.3495 grams); there are 12 Troy ounces to a Troy pound of 373.242 grams (the standard pound of 16 ounces is 453.592 grams). The Troy ounce divides into 20 pennyweight (abbreviated 'dwt').

From ancient times, gold has been valued for its own sake and widely used for coinage and jewellery. Gold was used as the basis for valuing all currencies under what was known as the 'gold standard'. This was abandoned by the UK in 1919, though reinstated in 1925 before final abandonment in 1931. Gold was removed from the articles of the International Monetary Fund in 1976.

Though the importance of gold has waned this century, its life is far from over. Gold is still used to settle international debts, and remains a popular investment. The price of gold is usually quoted in dollars per Troy ounce.

3.13 Other measures

There are innumerable other economic measures, whose importance can only be determined subjectively. Some of the commoner ones are:

Tax and prices index (TPI). This is the Retail Price Index but adjusted to show also the effects of taxation on people's incomes. It was introduced by the Conservative government soon after it took office in 1979 to dampen down demands for pay increases by showing the benefits of tax cuts. The principles used to calculate the TPI are questionable. Although the TPI is still produced, little use is made of it.

Government indices. Government departments (and others) produce so many statistics and indices that monthly books of them are published. These include banking statistics from the Bank of England, output indices produced by the Central Statistical Office, and the Index of Retail Sales produced by the Department of Trade and Industry.

[53]

Unemployment. The number of people unemployed affects the economy in two main ways: first, it is a measure of economic activity (or inactivity); second, high unemployment imposes a heavy burden on the national economy in the payment of unemployment benefit and other social security. The importance of the first factor depends on how far you subscribe to the philosophy of Keynesian economics.

Oil. Oil is a sufficiently important part of the country's and the world's economies to justify its own economic measure. Oil is traditionally valued in dollars per barrel; a barrel is 35 UK gallons (42 US gallons). North Sea Oil is usually quoted at the rate from Brent oilfields payable at 15 days. The Royal Bank of Scotland produces an oil production index.

LIBOR. Banks borrow and lend money to each other at a rate known as the Inter-Bank Offered Rate (IBOR). In London, this is known as the London Inter-Bank Offered Rate (LIBOR). The rate used for deposits is known as the Inter-Bank Market Bid Rate (IBBR). These rates change continuously during dealing hours, effectively providing an undercurrent to the banks' base rates, thus establishing them as an economic measure beyond their original purpose. The most commonly quoted rate is the 3-month inter-bank closing rate (i.e. what rate of interest one bank will charge another for a loan repayable in 3 months' time).

$$\boxed{4}$$

INTEREST CALCULATIONS

4.1 Simple and compound interest

Interest is a percentage which is applied to a sum of money over a period of time. One of its commonest uses is in calculating the amount of money earned on a sum deposited in a bank. The original amount deposited is called the principal.

On a simple interest basis, if the interest rate is 12 per cent and £100 is left on deposit a year, the interest will be £12. If it is left on deposit for 2 years, the interest will be £24. If left on deposit for 6 months it will be £6. Simple interest is still used in a few cases, such as certificates of tax deposit, but compound interest is now more commonly used.

With compound interest, the £100 on deposit at 12 per cent still grows to £112 after 1 year. However, for the following year the 12 per cent applies to the increased sum of £112, so the sum gross to £125.44. The principal has grown by £25.44 over 2 years, rather than the £24 under simple interest. The extra £1.44 is 12 per cent of the £12 interest earned in the first year.

The previous paragraph assumes that interest has been compounded annually. However, for all compound interest calculations we need to know how often the interest is to be calculated. We do not need to know that for simple interest calculations.

For most bank deposit accounts, interest is charged twice a year. So £100 at 12 per cent (i.e. 6 per cent every half year) would grow like this:

Principal	£100.00
6 months: add 6 per cent × £100 = £6	£106.00
12 months: add 6 per cent × £106 = £6.36	£112.36
18 months: add 6 per cent × £112.36 = £6.74	£119.10
24 months: add 6 per cent × £119.10 = £7.15	£126.25

If we apply the interest twice yearly instead of annually, the interest comes to £26.25: 81p more than if we applied it annually, and £2.25 more than if we used simple interest.

If we apply the interest rate monthly (at 1 per cent), the sum grows like this:

Principal £100.00

Month 1: £101.00	Month 9: £109.37	Month 17: £118.43
Month 2: £102.01	Month 10: £110.46	Month 18: £119.61
Month 3: £103.03	Month 11: £111.57	Month 19: £120.81
Month 4: £104.06	Month 12: £112.68	Month 20: £122.02
Month 5: £105.10	Month 13: £113.81	Month 21: £123.24
Month 6: £106.15	Month 14: £114.95	Month 22: £124.47
Month 7: £107.21	Month 15: £116.09	Month 23: £125.72
Month 8: £108.29	Month 16: £117.26	Month 24: £126.97

Our £100 at 12 per cent has grown over 2 years according to how the rate of interest has been applied, thus:

simple interest	£124.00
compound interest, annually	£125.44
compound interest, twice yearly	£126.25
compound interest, monthly	£126.97

These differences of a few pence become much more important over long periods:

	5 years	10 years	20 years	50 years	100 years
simple interest	160.00	220.00	340.00	700.00	1,300
compound, annual	176.23	310.58	964.63	28900.22	8,352,227
compound, twice yearly	179.08	320.71	1028.57	33930.21	11,512,590
compound, monthly	181.67	330.04	1089.26	39158.34	15,333,756

A curious fact about compound interest is that if you deal with periods shorter than the interval rate, compound interest produces *lower* amounts than simple interest:

[56]

	3 months	*6 months*	*9 months*
simple interest	103.00	106.00	109.00
compound, annual	102.87	105.83	108.87
compound, twice yearly	102.96	106.00	109.13
compound, monthly	103.03	106.15	109.37

Table 4.1 shows how compound interest can grow. To find out how much £160 will grow at 7 per cent interest for 6 years, for example, you read the factor for 6 years under 7 per cent, 1.5007, and multiply this by the principal: £160 × 1.5007 = £240.11.

If interest is charged every 6 months, multiply the number of years by 2 and use half the annual percentage rate. So for 7 per cent compounded every 6 months for 5 years, you take the factor for 3½ per cent for 10 years.

TABLE 4.1   Compound interest

Year	1%	1½%	2%	2½%	3%	3½%	4%	4½%
1	1.0100	1.0150	1.0200	1.0250	1.0300	1.0350	1.0400	1.0450
2	1.0201	1.0302	1.0404	1.0506	1.0609	1.0712	1.0816	1.0920
3	1.0303	1.0457	1.0612	1.0769	1.0927	1.1087	1.1249	1.1412
4	1.0406	1.0614	1.0824	1.1038	1.1255	1.1475	1.1699	1.1925
5	1.0510	1.0773	1.1041	1.1314	1.1593	1.1877	1.2167	1.2462
6	1.0615	1.0934	1.1262	1.1597	1.1941	1.2293	1.2653	1.3023
7	1.0721	1.1098	1.1487	1.1887	1.2299	1.2723	1.3159	1.3609
8	1.0829	1.1265	1.1717	1.2184	1.2668	1.3168	1.3686	1.4221
9	1.0937	1.1434	1.1951	1.2489	1.3048	1.3629	1.4233	1.4861
10	1.1046	1.1605	1.2190	1.2801	1.3439	1.4106	1.4802	1.5530
11	1.1157	1.1779	1.2434	1.3121	1.3842	1.4600	1.5395	1.6229
12	1.1269	1.1956	1.2682	1.3449	1.4258	1.5111	1.6010	1.6959
13	1.1381	1.2136	1.2936	1.3785	1.4685	1.5640	1.6651	1.7722
14	1.1495	1.2318	1.3195	1.4130	1.5126	1.6187	1.7317	1.8519
15	1.1610	1.2502	1.3459	1.4483	1.5580	1.6753	1.8009	1.9353
16	1.1726	1.2690	1.3728	1.4845	1.6047	1.7340	1.8730	2.0224
17	1.1843	1.2880	1.4002	1.5216	1.6528	1.7947	1.9479	2.1134
18	1.1961	1.3073	1.4282	1.5597	1.7024	1.8575	2.0258	2.2085
19	1.2081	1.3270	1.4568	1.5987	1.7535	1.9225	2.1068	2.3079
20	1.2202	1.3469	1.4859	1.6386	1.8061	1.9898	2.1911	2.4177

Year	5%	5½%	6%	6½%	7%	7½%	8%	8½%
1	1.0500	1.0550	1.0600	1.0650	1.0700	1.0750	1.0800	1.0850
2	1.1025	1.1130	1.1236	1.1342	1.1449	1.1556	1.1664	1.1772
3	1.1577	1.1742	1.1910	1.2079	1.2250	1.2423	1.2597	1.2773
4	1.2155	1.2388	1.2625	1.2865	1.3108	1.3355	1.3605	1.3859
5	1.2763	1.3070	1.3382	1.3701	1.4026	1.4356	1.4693	1.5037
6	1.3401	1.3788	1.4185	1.4591	1.5007	1.5433	1.5869	1.6315
7	1.4071	1.4568	1.5036	1.5540	1.6058	1.6590	1.7138	1.7701
8	1.4775	1.5347	1.5938	1.6550	1.7182	1.7835	1.8509	1.9206

TABLE 4.1   Compound interest – *cont*

Year	5%	5½%	6%	6½%	7%	7½%	8%	8½%
9	1.5513	1.6191	1.6895	1.7626	1.8385	1.9172	1.9990	2.0839
10	1.6289	1.7081	1.7908	1.8871	1.9672	2.0610	2.1589	2.2610
11	1.7103	1.8021	1.8983	1.9992	2.1049	2.2156	2.3316	2.4532
12	1.7959	1.9012	2.0122	2.1291	2.2522	2.3817	2.5182	2.6617
13	1.8856	2.0058	2.1329	2.2675	2.4098	2.5604	2.7196	2.8879
14	1.9799	2.1116	2.2609	2.4149	2.5785	2.7524	2.9372	3.1334
15	2.0789	2.2325	2.3966	2.5718	2.7590	2.9588	3.1722	3.3997
16	2.1829	2.3553	2.5404	2.7390	2.9522	3.1808	3.4259	3.6887
17	2.2920	2.4848	2.6928	2.9170	3.1588	3.4193	3.7000	4.0023
18	2.4066	2.6515	2.8543	3.1067	3.3799	3.6758	3.9960	4.3425
19	2.5270	2.7656	3.0256	3.3086	3.6165	3.9515	4.3157	4.7116
20	2.6533	2.9178	3.2071	3.5236	3.8697	4.2448	4.6610	5.1120

Year	9%	9½%	10%	10½%	11%	11½%	12%	12½%
1	1.0900	1.0950	1.1000	1.1050	1.1100	1.1150	1.1200	1.1250
2	1.1881	1.1990	1.2100	1.2210	1.2321	1.2432	1.2544	1.2656
3	1.2950	1.3129	1.3310	1.3492	1.3676	1.3862	1.4049	1.4238
4	1.4116	1.4377	1.4641	1.4909	1.5181	1.5456	1.5735	1.6018
5	1.5386	1.5742	1.6105	1.6474	1.6851	1.7234	1.7623	1.8020
6	1.6771	1.7328	1.7716	1.8204	1.8704	1.9215	1.9738	2.0273
7	1.8280	1.8876	1.9487	2.0116	2.0762	2.1425	2.2107	2.2807
8	1.9926	2.0669	2.1436	2.2228	2.3045	2.3889	2.4760	2.5658
9	2.1719	2.2632	2.3579	2.4562	2.5580	2.6636	2.7731	2.8865
10	2.3674	2.4782	2.5937	2.7141	2.8394	2.9699	3.1058	3.2473
11	2.5804	2.7137	2.8531	2.9991	3.1518	3.3115	3.4786	3.6532
12	2.8127	2.9715	3.1384	3.3140	3.4985	3.6923	3.8960	4.1099
13	3.0658	3.2537	3.4523	3.6619	3.8833	4.1169	4.3635	4.6236
14	3.3417	3.5629	3.7975	4.0464	4.3104	4.5904	4.8871	5.2016
15	3.3425	3.9013	4.1772	4.4713	4.7846	5.1183	5.4736	5.8518
16	3.9703	4.2719	4.5950	4.9408	5.3109	5.7069	6.1304	6.5833
17	4.3276	5.6778	5.0545	5.4596	5.8951	6.3632	6.8660	7.4062
18	4.7171	5.1222	5.5599	6.0328	6.5436	7.0949	7.6900	8.3319
19	5.1417	5.6088	6.1159	6.6673	7.2633	7.9108	8.6128	9.3734
20	5.6044	6.1416	6.7275	7.3362	8.0623	8.8206	9.6463	10.5451

Year	13%	13½%	14%	14½%	15%	15½%	16%	16½%
1	1.1300	1.1350	1.1400	1.1450	1.1500	1.1550	1.1600	1.1650
2	1.2769	1.2882	1.2996	1.3110	1.3255	1.3340	1.3456	1.3572
3	1.4429	1.4621	1.4815	1.5011	1.5209	1.5408	1.5609	1.5812
4	1.6305	1.6595	1.6890	1.7188	1.7490	1.7796	1.8106	1.8421
5	1.8424	1.8836	1.9254	1.9680	2.0114	2.0555	2.1003	2.1460
6	2.0820	2.1378	2.1950	2.2534	2.3131	2.3741	2.4364	2.5001
7	2.3526	2.4264	2.5023	2.5801	2.6600	2.7420	2.8262	2.9126
8	2.6584	2.7540	2.8526	2.9542	3.0590	3.1671	3.2784	3.3932
9	3.0040	3.1258	3.2519	3.3826	3.5179	3.6580	3.8030	3.9531
10	3.3946	3.5478	3.7072	3.8731	4.0456	4.2249	4.4114	4.6053
11	3.8359	4.0267	4.2262	4.4347	4.6524	4.8798	5.1173	5.3652
12	4.3385	4.5704	4.8179	5.0777	5.3508	5.6362	5.9360	6.2504
13	4.8980	5.1874	5.4924	5.8140	6.1528	6.5098	6.8858	7.2818
14	5.5348	5.8877	6.2613	6.6570	7.0757	7.5188	7.9875	8.4833
15	6.2543	6.6825	7.1379	7.6222	8.1371	8.6842	9.2655	9.8830
16	7.0673	7.5846	8.1372	8.7275	9.3576	10.0302	10.7480	11.5137
17	7.9861	8.6085	9.2765	9.9929	10.7613	11.5849	12.4677	13.4135

Year	13%	13½%	14%	14½%	15%	15½%	16%	16½%
18	9.0243	9.7707	10.5752	11.4419	12.3754	13.3806	14.4625	15.6267
19	10.1974	11.0897	12.0557	13.1010	14.2318	15.4546	16.7765	18.2051
20	11.5231	12.5869	13.7435	15.0006	16.3665	17.8501	19.4608	21.2089

4.2 Rule of 72

From Table 4.1 you will notice that eventually a sum of money doubles, trebles or even becomes ten or twenty times its original value.

A useful rule of thumb is known as the rule of 72. It says that if you divide 72 by the interest rate (in per cent), that will tell you how many years it takes for the money to double at that rate. Alternatively you can divide 72 by the number of years to find out at what interest rate it will double.

So, for an interest rate of 6 per cent, it takes 12 years for the money to double. Alternatively you could ask at what rate the money would double over 8 years, and the answer is 9 per cent (72 ÷ 8).

This also measures the effect of inflation. If inflation is running at 4 per cent, it takes 18 years for prices to double. If it is running at 24 per cent (about the highest recorded in the UK), prices double every 3 years.

If you want to know how long it takes for an amount to treble its size, you use 120 instead of 72.

Other factors are:

Money to grow by	Factor
1¼	22½
1½	42
1¾	58
2	72
2½	100
3	120
3½	140
4	156
5	180
6	200

[59]

This method gives useful approximations, but does not give an exact answer. To find the exact answer you must use one of these formulae:

$$A = \left[1 + \left(\frac{r}{100}\right)\right]^n$$

$$r = 100\,(n\sqrt{\bar{A}} - 1)$$

$$n = \frac{\log. \quad A}{\log. \; (1 + r/100)}$$

where A is the number of times by which the money (principal) increases, r is the rate of interest (per cent), and n is the number of years.

Table 4.2 indicates how long it takes for a principal to increase to a multiple of itself at given interest rates. For example, a sum will grow to five times its value at 9 per cent interest in 19 years.

4.3 Grossing up and netting down

If we take 20 per cent off £100 we have £80. Suppose we have the figure of £80 and want to know what figure less 20 per cent gives us £80. If we try just to add on 20 per cent we get £80 + £16 = £96. We are £4 out, because we are applying the percentage to a lower figure. We need a larger percentage to compensate, in this case 25 per cent added to £80 to get to £100, from which 20 per cent discount gives us £80. The 25 per cent is the 'grossed up' equivalent to 20 per cent.

The position is similar if we subtract. If we add 20 per cent to £100 we have £120. Suppose we want to know what percentage we must deduct to get back to the £100. If we try to subtract 20 per cent, we get £120 − £24 = £96. We are £4 out, because we are now taking 20 per cent of a higher figure. The correct percentage we need is lower. In this case the percentage is 16.67 per cent (to two decimal places). This is the 'netted down' equivalent to 20 per cent.

The formulae for calculating grossed up (GU) percentages and (ND) percentages from a percentage (P) are:

TABLE 4.2   Growth of principal (years)

Multiple	1%	2%	3%	4%	5%	6%	7%	8%	9%	10%	11%	12%	13%	14%	15%	16%	17%	18%	19%
1¼	22	11	7.6	5.7	4.6	3.8	3.3	2.9	2.6	2.3	2.1	2.0	1.8	1.7	1.6	1.5	1.4	1.4	1.3
1½	41	20	14	10	8.3	7.0	6.0	5.3	4.7	4.3	3.9	3.6	3.3	3.1	2.9	2.7	2.6	2.5	2.3
1¾	56	28	19	14	11	9.6	8.3	7.3	6.5	5.9	5.4	4.9	4.6	4.3	4.0	3.8	3.6	3.4	3.2
2	70	35	23	18	14	12	10	9.0	8.0	7.3	6.6	6.1	5.7	5.3	5.0	4.7	4.4	4.2	4.0
2½	92	46	31	23	19	16	14	12	11	9.6	8.8	8.1	7.5	7.0	6.6	6.2	5.8	5.5	5.3
3	110	55	37	28	23	19	16	14	13	12	11	9.7	9.0	8.4	7.9	7.4	7.0	6.6	6.3
4	139	70	47	35	28	24	20	18	16	15	13	12	11	11	9.9	9.3	8.8	8.4	8.0
5	162	81	54	41	33	28	24	21	19	17	15	14	13	12	12	11	10	9.7	9.3
6	180	90	61	46	37	31	26	23	21	19	17	16	15	14	13	12	11	11	10
7	196	98	66	50	40	33	29	25	23	20	19	17	16	15	14	13	12	12	11
8	209	105	70	53	43	36	31	27	24	22	20	18	17	16	15	14	13	13	12
9	221	111	74	56	45	38	32	29	26	23	21	19	18	17	16	15	14	13	13
10	231	116	78	59	47	40	34	30	27	24	22	20	19	18	16	16	15	14	13
15	272	137	92	69	56	46	40	35	31	28	26	24	22	21	19	18	17	16	16
20	301	151	101	76	61	51	44	39	35	31	29	26	25	23	21	20	19	18	17
25	324	163	109	82	66	55	48	42	37	34	31	28	26	25	23	22	21	19	19
30	342	172	115	87	70	58	50	44	40	36	33	30	28	26	24	23	22	21	20
40	371	186	125	94	76	63	55	48	43	39	35	33	30	28	26	25	24	22	21
50	393	198	132	100	80	67	58	51	45	41	38	35	32	30	28	26	25	24	23
100	463	233	156	117	94	79	68	60	53	48	44	41	38	35	33	31	29	28	27

$$GU = \frac{P}{100 - P}$$

$$ND = \frac{P}{100 + P}$$

Grossing up is often used in commerce. A customer requires 30 per cent discount on a product, so what must its retail price be if the wholesale price is £120? We gross it up 42.857 per cent to £171.42 (120 × 1.42857.)

Netting down is useful for finding out the VAT in an inclusive price. How much VAT at 15 per cent is there in a total bill of £10? We take 13.04347 per cent to give us £1.30. (For VAT at 15 per cent multiplying by $\frac{3}{23}$ is more accurate.)

Other grossing up and netting down figures are given in Table 4.3.

TABLE 4.3   Grossing up and netting down

%	Gross up	Net down	%	Gross up	Net down
1	1.01010	0.99010	16	19.04761	13.79310
1½	1.52284	1.47783	17	20.48192	14.52991
2	2.04081	1.96078	18	21.95122	15.25423
2½	2.56410	2.43902	19	23.45679	15.96638
3	3.09278	2.91262	20	25.00000	16.66667
3½	3.62694	3.38164	21	26.58227	17.35537
4	4.16667	3.84615	22	28.20512	18.03278
4½	4.71204	4.30622	23	29.87013	18.69918
5	5.26315	4.76190	24	31.57894	19.35483
5½	5.82010	5.21327	25	33.33333	20.00000
6	6.28297	5.66037	26	35.13513	20.63492
6½	6.95187	6.10328	27	36.98630	21.25984
7	7.52688	6.54205	28	38.88889	21.87500
7½	8.10811	6.97674	29	40.84507	22.48062
8	8.69565	7.40740	30	42.85714	23.07692
8½	9.28961	7.83410	31	44.92753	23.66412
9	9.89010	8.25688	32	47.05882	24.24242
9½	10.49723	8.67579	33	49.25373	24.81203
10	11.11111	9.09091	34	51.51515	25.37313
10½	11.73184	9.50226	35	53.84615	25.92592
11	12.35955	9.90990	36	56.25000	26.47058
11½	12.99435	10.31390	37	58.73015	27.00729
12	13.63637	10.71428	38	61.29032	27.53623
12½	14.28571	11.11111	39	63.93442	28.05755
13	14.94252	11.50442	40	66.66667	28.57142
13½	15.60694	11.89427	45	81.81818	31.03448
14	16.27907	12.28070	50	100.00000	33.33333
14½	16.95906	12.66376	75	300.00000	42.85714
15	17.64705	13.04347	100	infinity	50.00000

4.4 Discounted cashflow

Cashflow is the recording of when money comes in and goes out. A company which buys a machine for hire might see a cashflow like this:

Years			Balance
1:	Outflow (purchase)	£4000	(£4000)
	Hire fees	£100	(£3900)
2:	Hire fees	£500	(£3400)
3:	Hire fees	£600	(£2800)
	Repairs	£50	(£2850)
4:	Hire fees	£800	(£2050)
	Repairs	£60	(£2110)
5:	Hire fees	£1000	(£1110)
	Repairs	£100	(£1210)
6:	Hire fees	£1200	(£10)
	Repairs	£150	(£160)
7:	Hire fees	£800	£640
	Repairs	£300	£340
8:	Hire fees	£500	£840
	Repairs	£400	£440

After year 8 the company realises that the machine is getting a bit old. The repair fees have nearly increased to the amount earned in hire fees, so the machine is scrapped. But we have earned £440 more than we have spent, so that is fine. Or is it?

It is not until year 7 that the machine has earned enough to pay for itself, and by this time our pounds are worth less than when we started. We have not allowed for the effects of inflation, the cost of capital or the interest we had to pay to borrow the money to pay for the thing in the first place.

We get round this by using the discounted cashflow. For each year we multiply the inflows and outflows by a factor which reflects inflation, cost of capital or interest payments.

Suppose we decide that we need to use the rate of inflation, which we expect to be 5 per cent over the period. That means that for year 2 the cashflows will only be worth 100/105 of what they were in year 1. In year 3 the cashflows

[63]

will only be worth $100^2/105^2$ of what they would have been in year 1. These factors can easily be worked out on a calculator, but are usually taken from a table of discounted cashflow factors.

Using a rate of 5 per cent our cashflow becomes a discounted cashflow thus:

Year		Amount	Factor	DCF amount	Balance
1	Outflow (purchase)	£4000	1.0000	£4000.00	(£4000.00)
	Hire fees	£100	1.0000	£100.00	(£3900.00)
2	Hire fees	£500	0.9524	£476.20	(£3423.80)
3	Hire fees	£600	0.9070	£544.20	(£2879.60)
	Repairs	£50	0.9070	£45.35	(£2924.95)
4	Hire fees	£800	0.8638	£691.04	(£2233.91)
	Repairs	£60	0.8638	£51.83	(£2285.74)
5	Hire fees	£1000	0.8227	£822.70	(£1463.04)
	Repairs	£100	0.8227	£82.27	(£1545.31)
6	Hire fees	£1200	0.7835	£940.20	(£605.11)
	Repairs	£150	0.7835	£117.53	(£722.64)
7	Hire fees	£800	0.7462	£596.96	(£125.68)
	Repairs	£300	0.7462	£223.86	(£349.54)
8	Hire fees	£500	0.7107	£355.35	£5.81
	Repairs	£400	0.7107	£284.28	(£278.47)

Now that we have allowed for the effect of 5 per cent inflation, our 'profit' of £440 has become a loss of £278.47, for when we earn the money, it is worth less than when we spent it. £1 in year 8 is only worth 71p in year 1. When we adjust something for the effect of inflation we describe the figure as being 'in real terms'.

Other discount factors are given in Table 4.4.

TABLE 4.4   Discount factors

Year	1%	2%	3%	4%	5%	6%	7%	8%
1	1.0000	1.0000	1.0000	1.0000	1.0000	1.0000	1.0000	1.0000
2	0.9901	0.9804	0.9709	0.9615	0.9524	0.9434	0.9346	0.9259
3	0.9803	0.9612	0.9426	0.0246	0.9070	0.8900	0.8734	0.8573
4	0.9706	0.9423	0.9151	0.8890	0.8638	0.8396	0.8163	0.7939
5	0.9610	0.9239	0.8885	0.8548	0.8227	0.7921	0.7629	0.7350
6	0.9515	0.9057	0.8626	0.8219	0.7835	0.7473	0.7130	0.6806
7	0.9420	0.8880	0.8375	0.7903	0.7462	0.7050	0.6663	0.6302
8	0.9327	0.8706	0.8139	0.7599	0.7107	0.6651	0.6228	0.5835
9	0.9235	0.8535	0.7894	0.7307	0.6768	0.6274	0.5820	0.5403
10	0.9143	0.8368	0.7664	0.7026	0.6446	0.5919	0.5439	0.5003

Year	9%	10%	11%	12%	13%	14%	15%	16%
1	1.0000	1.0000	1.0000	1.0000	1.0000	1.0000	1.0000	1.0000
2	0.9174	0.9091	0.9009	0.8929	0.8850	0.8772	0.8696	0.8621
3	0.8417	0.8265	0.8116	0.7972	0.7832	0.7695	0.7561	0.7432
4	0.7722	0.7513	0.7312	0.7118	0.6931	0.6750	0.6575	0.6407
5	0.7084	0.6830	0.6587	0.6355	0.6133	0.5921	0.5718	0.5523
6	0.6499	0.6209	0.5935	0.5674	0.5428	0.5194	0.4972	0.4762
7	0.5963	0.5645	0.5346	0.5066	0.4803	0.4556	0.4324	0.4105
8	0.5470	0.5132	0.4817	0.4524	0.4251	0.3996	0.3760	0.3539
9	0.5019	0.4665	0.4339	0.4039	0.3762	0.3506	0.3270	0.3051
10	0.4604	0.4241	0.3909	0.3605	0.3329	0.3075	0.2844	0.2630

4.5 Annualised percentage rates

If you borrow £1,200 at 10 per cent interest for 3 years, you will repay £1,200 plus 30 per cent interest to give a total repayment of £1,560. Suppose the lender is not prepared to wait to the end of the 3-year period for all his money, but wants it in three annual instalments of £520.

Each of these instalments is effectively a £400 repayment of the original loan plus £120 interest. At the end of the first year when you pay £520, you are paying interest of £120 on £400, which you have only borrowed for 1 year. That means you are actually paying 30 per cent interest on that payment.

In year 2 you pay £120 interest on £400 that you have then borrowed for 2 years. That is a rate of 15 per cent interest. Only in year 3 is your interest rate the 10 per cent actually quoted, because it is only on the last payment that you have actually borrowed that bit of the loan for the whole period. The principle is that when you make payments on a loan before the end, you are paying a higher rate of interest than the annual rate which you use for the calculations.

The Consumer Credit Act 1974 requires that all finance agreements must quote the rate of interest charged as a annualised percentage rate or APR. This is calculated from the annual rate by this formula:

$$A = 100\left[(1 + (\frac{x}{100m})y - 1\right]$$

where x is the annual rate (per cent), y is the number of years of the agreement, and m is the number of periods in the year in which the interest is charged (1 if annually, 12 if monthly, 52 if weekly).

In our example above, the APR is 33.1 per cent.

If you want to know the amount which is actually being charged, you compare APRs. If you actually want to calculate the interest, you use the annual rate.

FINANCIAL ACCOUNTING

5.1 Accounting statements

Almost all trading activities produce two accounting statements:

1 balance sheet,
2 profit and loss account.

The balance sheet is like a snapshot. It reflects the position of the company at one moment in time. That moment is often the close of business on the last day of the company's financial year, but can be at any other time. It lists what a company has, what it owes and how the balance is 'funded'.

The profit and loss account is a history. It covers a period of time and shows you what the company did in that period.

So a balance sheet is described as 'balance sheet as at [date]', while a profit and loss account is described as 'profit and loss for the year ended [date]', except that the period covered need not always be a year.

5.2 Balance sheet

Suppose a company issues £1,000,000 worth of shares to buy a factory for £400,000, equipment for £350,000, and stock (for resale) for £50,000, and still has £200,000 in cash.

It collects £1,000,000 from people who are now its share-holders. When that has been done, its balance sheet would look like this:

Cash	£200,000
Stock	£50,000
Equipment	£350,000
Factory	£400,000
	£1,000,000

Funded by:
Share capital   £1,000,000

Notice that the first list and the 'represented by' figures must be the same. That is they must balance, hence the name balance sheet.

The company then sells £10,000 worth of stock for £12,000 (making £2,000 profit). The balance sheet now looks like this:

Cash	£212,000	[£200,000 + £12,000]
Stock	£40,000	[£50,000 − £10,000]
Equipment	£350,000	
Factory	£400,000	
	£1,002,000	

Funded by:

Share capital	£1,000,000	
Profit	£2,000	[£12,000 − £10,000]
	£1,002,000	

The figures still balance, but now the company is worth £2000 more because it has made a profit.

The company sells another £5,000 worth of stock for £6,000 (making another £1,000 profit), but this time the customer does not pay cash but owes the money.

The balance sheet will now look like this:

Cash	£212,000	
Debtors	£6,000	[0 + £6,000]
Stock	£35,000	[£40,000 − £5,000]
Equipment	£350,000	
Factor	£400,000	
	£1,003,000	

Funded by:

Share capital	£1,000,000	
Profit	£3,000	[£2,000 + £1,000]
	£1,003,000	

The company now buys another £20,000 worth of stock. The balance sheet becomes:

Cash	£192,000	[£212,000 − £20,000]
Debtors	£6,000	
Stock	£55,000	[£35,000 + £20,000]
Equipment	£350,000	
Factory	£400,000	
	£1,003,000	

Funded by:

Share capital	£1,000,000	
Profit	£3,000	
	£1,003,000	

The company buys £10,000 more equipment, but does not yet pay for it. The balance sheet becomes:

Cash	£192,000	
Debtors	£6,000	
Stock	£65,000	[£55,000 + £10,000]
Equipment	£350,000	
Factory	£400,000	
	£1,013,000	
Less creditors	£10,000	
	£1,003,000	

[69]

Funded by:
    Share capital   £1,000,000
    Profit   £3,000
                      £1,003,000

We could carry on like this for ever, redrawing a balance sheet every time we bought something, sold something, collected a debt, paid a bill or made any other kind of financial transaction. However, this would quickly become very tedious, even in a very small business, so the procedure is streamlined by double-entry bookkeeping. But before coming to that, we need to understand about assets and liabilities.

5.3   Assets and liabilities

An asset is:

1   money,
2   something that is worth money (e.g. stock, furniture, buildings),
3   something that will become money (e.g. debtors),
4   something that will save you money (prepayments).

The ease with which the asset can be turned into money is called its liquidity. Cash is obviously the most liquid asset of all. Sums deposited in the bank are not far behind. For debts you may have to wait weeks or months before you see the money, so they are less liquid. Stock has first to be sold to produce a debt to produce cash, so that is even less liquid. Your factory, furniture and machinery will probably never directly produce cash at all, though clearly worth money, so they are the least liquid assets of all.

If an asset is expected to become money within 1 year, it is called a *current asset*. Otherwise it is (generally) called a *fixed asset*.

The opposite to an asset is a liability. A liability is someone to whom you owe money, your creditors. If you must pay the money within 1 year, it is a *current liability*. If you must pay it in more than 1 year's time, it is a *long-term liability*.

5.4   Capital employed

All the assets less all the liabilities give the company's *capital employed*. This is made up of three things:

1   equity capital,
2   borrowed capital,
3   retained profit.

Equity capital is the original money put in by the shareholders (or partners or proprietor). If shareholders have added more capital after the business started becoming profitable, they will probably have had to pay extra for their shares. This is known as the *share premium*, which is shown separately but is still part of the equity capital.

Borrowed capital comprises debentures, and loan stock.

Preference shares combine elements of equity capital and loan capital. They are loan capital in that the dividend is usually a fixed percentage rather than a share of profits. They are equity capital in that if the profit is insufficient, it may be possible that no dividend at all is paid.

Retained profit is simply the balance of past profits that the business has not paid out to its shareholders (or partners or proprietor) but kept for the business. Strictly, retained profit is part of a business's equity capital, but is always shown separately.

5.5   Double-entry bookkeeping

In accounting, each sum of money is represented in the books by either a debit or a credit.

A debit is used to represent:

1   an asset,
2   an expense,
3   losses,
4   the reduction of a liability.

A credit is used to represent the opposite, namely:

1   a liability,
2   income,
3   profits,
4   the reduction in value of an asset.

This might seem an odd breakdown, but it means that every financial transaction can be represented by debits and credits for the same total amount.
  Here are some examples:

	DEBIT	CREDIT
You sell a product for cash:	Cash	Income
You sell a product on credit:	Debtors	Income
You buy stock for cash:	Stock	Cash
You buy stock on credit:	Stock	Creditors
A customer pays your bill:	Cash	Debtors
You pay a bill:	Creditors	Cash
You receive the electricity bill:	Expenses	Creditors
You pay your staff:	Wages	Cash
You buy some furniture for cash:	Fixed assets	Cash
You buy furniture on credit:	Fixed assets	Creditors

Sometimes there may be more than one debit or credit, particularly when tax comes into it. For example paying wages to staff in practice will call for:

DEBIT	CREDIT
Wages payable	Cash [amount actually given to staff]
Employer's national insurance	Creditor [income tax and NI]

Similarly an invoice issued by a trader registered for VAT calls for the following entries:

DEBIT	CREDIT
Debtors	Income
	Creditor [VAT]

But in all cases all the debits of one transaction must equal all its credits.

5.6 Day books

For convenience these debits and credits are listed in day books. The usual day books are:

1 sales day book (records all invoices issued by the business),
2 purchase day book (records all invoices and bills received by the business),
3 cash book (records all payments in and out of a bank account – there is usually one cash book for every bank account),
4 petty cash book (a cash book for the loose cash kept on the premises),
5 wages book (records the payroll),
6 journal (records everything else).

A company may also have expenses day books and subsidiary sales or purchase day books for parts of its business. Some companies may not need all these day books. Nowadays the 'books' often take the form of computer software, but the principles are still exactly the same.

All books of account must bear a unique reference, known as the folio, so that an entry can be traced from one stage in the accounting process to another. The books of account are periodically summarised, and the summaries are entered as double entries in the nominal ledger, from which the final accounts are prepared.

Some balances may be supported by ledgers. For example, the balance for debtors may be supported by a sales ledger. Such a ledger is not part of the double-entry system.

5.7 Journal

The journal is used to write all the double entries that cannot easily be recorded in another day book. It has two columns marked 'DR' and 'CR' for 'debit' and 'credit'. ('DR' comes from the Italian word *dare*, to give, used in the first double-entry books of Genoan traders in 1340.)

Typically the journal is used to:

1 open a new set of books,
2 record the end of year stock valuation,
3 record depreciation on fixed assets,
4 record accruals and prepayments, and reverse them in the following period,
5 make provisions and reserves (such as audit fee, doubtful debts, contingencies and proposed dividends),
6 record the corporation tax or income tax liability,
7 write off any amount,
8 correct errors found in any prime books of account,
9 record unusual accounting transactions.

Depreciation is the cost of using a fixed asset. If an asset costing £5,000 is expected to last for 5 years, the company may choose to write off £1,000 a year in depreciation. When purchased, the asset would have been recorded in the cash day book – DR asset: CR cash (or creditors). The asset would be shown on the balance sheet at £5,000. The depreciation charge would be recorded in the journal – DR depreciation; CR asset – and the asset would be shown in the balance sheet at £4,000.

5.8   Realisation of profit

A man buys 100 widgets for £20 each. He sells them for £30 each, sending out an invoice with each one. Some time later, the customer pays for them.

At what point has the widget-seller made his profit?

Usually the answer is the second stage, when the sale has been made. Before then, there is some doubt that anyone may buy them. The profit has not been 'realised'.

The expenses of the business are adjusted so that only those which were incurred in the same period are shown in the accounts. The expenses are said to be 'matched' against the profit. This, broadly, is known as the *accruals basis*.

[74]

Sometimes the seller will only take the profit when the customer has actually paid for the goods. This is known as the *cash basis*. The cash basis is normally used for administrative convenience rather than because of the nature of the business.

Sometimes a basis halfway between the accruals and cash basis is used. This is known as the *conventional basis*. The profit may be realised when certain documents are despatched, for example. The conventional basis is often used in the construction industry.

5.9 Profit

The excess of what a trader receives for his goods over what he paid for them is known as the *gross profit*. From his gross profit, he has expenses of being in business. These are known as overheads, and include such costs as rent, electricity, stationery and advertising. These overheads are subtracted from the gross profit to give the *net profit*.

Thus a profit and loss account can be shown in outline as:

- Sales − cost of sales = Gross profit
- Gross profit − overheads = Net profit.

Sometimes a business has sources of income other than its profit from trade. It may rent spare premises or have money invested. Therefore the business may distinguish between *operating profit* (or trading profit) and other sources of income (e.g. 'rent', 'investment income').

If the costs exceed the sales figure, the business has made a gross loss. If the business has overheads which exceeds any gross profit, it has made a net loss.

Note that only commercial bodies make a profit or a loss, and produce a profit and loss account. Non-commercial bodies (such as clubs, charities and churches) may make a *surplus* or *deficit*, as shown in an *income and expenditure account*.

[75]

5.10   Bad debts

If a customer does not pay an invoice, the company may regard it first as a *doubtful debt*, and later as a *bad debt*. It is becoming increasingly common not to bother with doubtful debts, and to move straight to bad debts.

A business *provides* for a doubtful debt but *writes off* a bad debt. There are two distinctions here:

1   a doubtful debt is still part of the business's profit; it is just shown separately. A bad debt is deducted from the profit.
2   Tax relief is given on a bad debt, but not on a doubtful debt.

5.11   Credit control

The process of ensuring that debts are paid is known as credit control. There are two separate stages to credit control: preventative and curative.

Preventative credit control is designed to ensure that bad debts do not arise in the first place. This can be done by proper taking up of references, and credit-vetting. Some businesses do not even observe their own sales ledger, and continue supplying customers of known uncreditworthiness.

It should be understood that supplying uncreditworthy customers is an extremely foolish policy. Suppose a business makes 10 per cent profit. It has the opportunity of supplying a doubtful customer with £100 worth of goods. If the customer pays, the business has made £10 profit. If the customer does not pay, it has made a £90 loss. The business must make another nine similar sales just to recoup the loss made on that one.

Curative credit control is debt-collecting, which is a bit of an art form. The credit controller should use a range of devices to secure payment, and should liaise with the sales department in deciding which ones to use.

Most customers who delay payment do so to subsidise their own cash position, not to defraud the supplier. If a customer is about to become insolvent, prompt and tough action is needed. If a customer is going through a difficult time, a more sympathetic approach is likely to be more fruitful.

The normal procedure is to send out a *statement* showing what is outstanding. This is followed up with letters, not containing threats but pressing for payment. These should be followed up by telephone calls to decide what, if any, further action is necessary. Further action can include stopping further supplies, legal action or a personal visit (or a combination).

Legal action usually means a county court summons for amounts up to £5,000, or a high court summons for amounts above. County court summonses can be issued by the business's own staff; high court proceedings need a solicitor. The proceedings lead to a judgment which then has to be enforced. This may be done by seizure of goods, attachment of earnings, bankruptcy or liquidation proceedings, distraint on property or an order to attend court.

5.12   Accounting standards

Accountancy is not a united profession in the way that the law and medicine are. There are several bodies with royal charters that are recognised for different purposes. For example, there are four accounting bodies recognised as auditors of limited companies – three comprising *chartered accountants* and one comprising *certified accountants*.

Published accounts in the UK are very subjective. They are designed to present a 'true and fair view' rather than a definitive statement of objective accuracy. Accounting standards in other countries, particularly West Germany and USA, are much more prescriptive: this is colloquially known as the 'cook book approach'.

The accounting bodies have joined together to publish accounting standards. These mainly comprise *Statements of Standard Accounting Practice* (SSAPs), of which there were twenty-three by the end of 1990.

SSAPs do not remove the subjectivity from accounts, but they do restrict it. Some of the less acceptable practices have

[77]

been outlawed. In many other areas where there is still a choice in approach, there is a requirement to disclose the procedure or method adopted.

SSAPs are mandatory on qualified accountants. An accountant who ignores the provisions of an SSAP could be disciplined by his professional body, though there has been no known example of this happening.

The bodies also publish *Statements of Recommended Practice* (SORPs), which are of the nature of guidance notes. There are also standards and guidelines for auditing.

The UK accounting bodies have joined with those of other countries to produce International Accounting Standards (IASs), which are not compulsory in the UK, though most SSAPs ensure compliance with them.

Examples of some specific accounting provisions in grey areas are given in the rest of this chapter.

5.13 Valuation

Valuation of assets can have a marked effect on a business's profitability. There are two main areas where valuation is critical.

The first is in a business's fixed assets, particularly land and buildings. If a company buys for £5 million a factory which is worth £8 million 3 years later, the value of that business has effectively grown by £3 million. This increase, known as a *revaluation surplus* is effectively additional profit, though subject to restrictions on its distribution to shareholders.

Up to the early 1970s it was common for businesses to have property vastly undervalued. This meant that the business could be bought cheaply, closed and the property sold at current market values for a quick profit. This rather anti-social behaviour is known as *asset-stripping*. It is now normal to revalue land and buildings every 3 years to avoid such problems.

The second main area is in stock valuation. The relevant SSAP requires stock to be valued at 'lower of cost or net realisable value'. So if you have some stock which you bought for £100, but you can only now sell it for £80 (per-

[78]

haps because it is damaged or out of fashion), and it costs you £10 to advertise it, the net realisable value is only £70.

5.14   Goodwill

Goodwill is the excess of a business's value over the value of its net assets.

If you add up the value of all the land, buildings, plant, equipment, stock and cash possessed by a business, you may come to a figure of, say, £20 million. However, you cannot buy the business for £20 million. The business may have a value of £25 million.

The extra £5 million is goodwill. It represents the value of such things as good customer relations, reputation, location, past advertising, expertise and staff loyalty. Sometimes the goodwill is expressed in terms of profit. If a business makes £1 million a year profit and the goodwill is £5 million, it is expressed as 5 years' profit. The goodwill is effectively seen as an investment paying 20 per cent a year 'interest'.

It should be noted that there are other intangible assets, such as patents, copyrights, scientific know-how and technological development. Where these can be valued separately, they should be excluded from goodwill and shown as separate items in the balance sheet.

A company is not allowed to show goodwill in its balance sheet. If it buys a business, any amount paid for goodwill must be written off against profit as soon as possible.

5.15   Contingencies

Contingencies are assets or liabilities whose outcome is unsure. For example, you may have admitted a legal liability, but do not know how much you will have to pay until the case is settled. The accounting standards generally require a contingent asset to be ignored in the accounts, but disclosed in a note to the accounts, and for a contingent liability to be stated at the maximum amount.

5.16 Audit

Under company law, all limited companies must be audited once a year. The auditor's statement must be published with the accounts.

The auditor is required to give an opinion on whether the accounts:

1 are true and fair, and
2 comply with the Companies Act 1985.

Note that it is not the auditor's job to check that the accounts are accurate. Nor is it his job to see whether any fiddles or frauds are going on or whether any other laws are being broken. If the auditor is not satisfied on any point he may give a *qualified report*. In an extreme case he may report that he is unable to form an opinion.

The texts of audit reports follow a set format, largely taken from auditing standards and guidelines produced by the accounting profession.

6

MANAGEMENT ACCOUNTING

6.1 Introduction

Financial accounting lets a business know how much profit or loss it has made, but it does not say *how* it was made. That is done by management accounting, which has invented not only special terms and formulae but a new item – the widget. What it is and who uses it remains unknown even though pages have been written about how much it costs.

At its simplest, management accounting measures profits simply by deducting the cost from the price. So if a widget costs £12 and we sell it for £15, the profit made on each widget is £3.

The problem is how do we cost the widget? There are basically three different costing methods, according to what we are trying to do:

1 direct costing, which is used for normal pricing, and deciding whether to sell an item,
2 marginal costing, which is used to decide whether to sell more of an item,
3 opportunity costing, which is used to make choices.

6.2 Direct costing

Direct costing adds up the elements of cost, which are usually classed under two general headings:

1 *Direct costs*, those items which can be related directly to a product,

[81]

2 *indirect costs* or *overheads*, those items which relate to running the business as a whole and which cannot easily be related directly to a product.

Sometimes direct costs are called *variable costs*, and indirect costs called *fixed costs*.

Direct costs are usually divided between materials and labour. Other things, such as electricity, could be directly related, but in practice it is preferable to regard such things as part of the general overhead.

For both materials and labour, we can calculate *budgeted costs* and *actual costs*. The budgeted material cost is the best price we pay for the material in the quantity in which we use it. The actual cost may be less, because we find a cheaper supplier or buy more and get a bitter quantity discount. It may be more, because we bought less than expected, the price went up or we had to buy from a dearer supplier for some reason.

The budgeted labour cost is how much we have to pay the workforce to process the materials to the finished product. This comprises the wages of the storeman who kits out the parts, machinists, assemblers and testers. For each of them the labour cost is a wage cost muliplied by a rate. Problems of labour costing are discussed further in section 6.7.

The wage rate is easy enough to find. The time can be ascertained in one of two ways. One is to take a competent worker and to time him while he does the work; this produces a *standard time*. The other is to break the job down into separate stages known as *synthetics* and to time those. For example, it takes the worker 30 seconds to pick up a resistor, 45 seconds to see where to solder it, 15 seconds to pick up his soldering iron, 25 seconds to pick up the solder, etc. The disadvantage of synthetics is that they allow no time for the worker to scratch his nose, cough, go to the loo, look out the window, and perform any other such activities. Synthetics tend to be used in specialist circumstances, while standard time is used more generally.

In the 1970s there were various incomes policies imposed as a means to combat inflation (or try to). The policies restricted the amount of pay rises that could be given. One way to get round this was to increase standard times, thus increasing the apparent productivity and consequently the productivity pay. Although the economic policy has long since disappeared, standard times may still be excessive for this reason.

One of the roles of the management accountant is to measure the *variance* between the budgeted and actual costs. The difference is referred to as *favourable* or *unfavourable*.

6.3 Overhead recovery

Every business has expenses which relate simply to being in business. These include rates, rent, administrative staff, stationery, telephone, marketing, electricity and suchlike. If a business sells 5,000 widgets at £15 each when each has a direct cost of £10, but has overheads of £40,000, it will make a loss. The gross profit of £25,000 from the sale of widgets will not cover the overheads of £40,000.

The problem is how to build into the direct cost an element of the overheads (or indirect costs). There are two common methods:

1 apportionment.
2 absorption.

Apportionment divides the overheads by the amount of production. In our example, we divide £40,000 by 5,000 items and add £8 *indirect cost* to the direct cost of £10. We then see that our *total cost* for a widget is £18 and that we make a loss if we sell it for £15. The disadvantage of such a method is discussed in section 6.4.

If a company makes more than one product, the apportionment is usually done on a pro rata basis. If the direct costs for all products amount to £30,000 and the overheads are £12,000, the direct cost is uplifted by 40 per cent (£12,000 + £30,000). If a product's direct cost is £20, its total cost becomes £28.

Absorption avoids total cost. It takes the difference

[83]

between the selling price and the total direct costs. This is known as the *contribution*, so that a widget is regarded as making a contribution of £5 towards the overheads of the business. From this the *breakeven* is calculated. If the overheads are £40,000 and the contribution per widget is £5, the breakeven is reached when 8,000 widgets (£40,000 ÷ £5) are sold.

6.4 Marginal costing

Our widgets have total direct and indirect costs of £18 each, and we can sell them for £24 each. We have the chance of an export order for 1,000 widgets, provided the price is no more than £15 each.

Using direct costing only, we would automatically say no – at £15 each we make a loss of £3 each. Or do we?

The figure of £18 includes £8 apportionment of overheads. But we don't have to pay any more rates just because we are making more widgets. Nor do we have to pay the accountant any more. All these costs have already been earned once from the first lot of sales, and don't have to be paid again. The cost of making an *extra* widget is simply the direct cost. In this example it costs us £10 to make an extra widget, on each of which we earn an extra £5 profit.

This assumes that we have sufficient ability to make the widgets within our existing resources. It is more likely that we shall have to pay overtime, engage more staff, rent more office space, etc. Conversely, buying more material may enable us to buy more cheaply. But such considerations turn our decision into an exercise in opportunity costing.

One of the disadvantages of apportionment is that we have to use a budgeted sales quantity. If we exceed that quantity, the direct cost is reduced; if we fail to meet it, the direct cost is increased. The export has increased our sales, but note that direct costing will still not give us the OK to accept our export order.

With the export order our cost budget becomes:

6,000 widgets with direct cost of £10 each	£60,000
overheads	£40,000
total	£100,000

Total cost per widget = £100,000 ÷ 6000 = £16.67.

According to direct costing we should still not accept the export order, even though we have already shown by marginal costing that we shall make an extra profit from doing so.

6.5 Opportunity costing

Sometimes the decision whether or not to do something confronts us with more choices than we have looked at so far. Alternatively the choice may bring to light more factors than we have considered so far.

For this we use *opportunity costing*. We base our decision on the basis of *the cost of the next best option*.

You have spent £400 on repairs to an old car. It still fails its MOT and it will cost another £500 to put it right; it will then be worth about £800. Do you proceed to spend £900 for something worth £800? The answer is yes, because the first £400 has already been spent and cannot be 'unspent'. Your choice is to spend £500 on repairs or £900 for an equivalent car. The £400 is irrelevant to the decision. It is called a *sunk cost* and is ignored in opportunity costing.

Imagine that we find in our stores a ton of sprogget-brass. This has sat there for 12 years because the production manager forgot to tell the chief buyer when the company stopped making sproggets. Our choice is that we could dump it or use it to make widgets.

If we use it to make widgets, what cost do we use? It cost us £1,000 12 years ago; if we add on inflation that becomes £3,500, but if we bought it today it would cost £5,000. The answer is that, like our car repair bill, the cost of the brass is a sunk cost, and we simply compare the cost of dumping the brass with the cost of using it to make widgets.

The cost may actually prove to be a profit. If we use the sprogget-brass to make widgets, that part of the material cost is zero, which may mean that we can sell our widgets for less and still cover the other costs.

6.6 Overview

For direct costing and marginal costing we have assumed that costs fall neatly into two classes: direct and indirect. This is convenient but ignores that, ultimately, all costs are a mixture of direct and indirect costs. If our production goes above certain limits, we shall need extra storage space, more inspectors and more racks to put it on. If the quantity of business increases, we shall need more stationery and more accounts staff and make more telephone calls.

In addition, the material cost could include a fixed charge for postage and packing. The cost of placing the order is a fixed indirect cost.

The distinction between direct and indirect costs therefore can become blurred. Sometimes it is necessary to split a cost into the two elements or account for them in a more sophisticated way.

It is also fair to point out that many management accounting terms are used interchangeably. In particular 'marginal costing' and 'direct costing' are often used to mean the same thing. However, definitions and terminology are less important than understanding the principles, and realising which method to use (and how to use it) to achieve a particular result.

6.7 Labour costs

Particular problems arise in costing labour time. If you employ a man for £8,000 a year and he has to work 7½ hours a day 5 days a week, you might think the matter is simple. He is contracted to work 1,950 hours (7½ × 5 × 52). At £8,000 a year that is £4.10 an hour (£8,000 ÷ 1,950).

Wrong! To start with he has holidays, perhaps 20 days a year, as well as the eight public holidays. That reduces his working days per year from 260 to 232, increasing his hourly rate from £4.10 to £4.59 (£8,000 ÷ 1,740). If he has ten days' paid sick leave, his hourly rate effectively increases to £4.80 (£8,000 ÷ 1,665).

We are still assuming that all the hours he attends are actually worked. The truth is different. He will turn up late, and spend time chatting about the midnight film, drinking coffee, waiting for things or for people, visiting the dentist (or pretending to), chatting up the secretaries, coming back late from the pub, sorting out his tools or files, arguing with his boss and so on. For office staff the hours actually engaged in work can be as few as 50 per cent, but for our example let us assume they are 70 per cent. The hourly rate now becomes £6.86 (£8,000 ÷ 1,165.5).

Our cost of employing him is not £8,000. We pay an extra 10.45 per cent in employer's national insurance and perhaps 2 per cent to a pension plan, and probably have other similar charges. That increases his annual cost to £8,996 and his hourly rate to £7.72 (£8,996 ÷ 1,165.5) – nearly double the figure we started with.

Many direct costs can be closely related to staff, and it may be regarded as appropriate for them to be built into the labour cost rather than left as part of the indirect cost. All this is before you allow for the costs attendant on health and safety, unfair dismissal, time off for trade union duties, maternity leave and many other legal requirements. Employing staff is very expensive.

6.8 Economic batch quantity

Management accounting does more than just determine costs. It leads into a whole branch of management mathematics which can be usefully employed to solve commercial problems. Only a few of these can be mentioned in this book.

One of them concerns how much of an item you should order. The more you order, the greater is your stockholding cost (e.g. lost interest on the money you have spent) but the less is your ordering cost for the item.

The total stockholding cost for a period of time (usually a year) is given by the formula:

[87]

$$T = \frac{Cd}{q} + \frac{ipq}{2}$$

where T = total stockholding cost for a year, C = the cost of placing an order, d = the annual demand (how many are used in a year), i = interest rate (usually cost of capital), p = cost of one item, and q = order quantity.

By algebra and calculus we can calculate the economic batch quantity (EBQ) to be:

$$EBQ = \sqrt{\frac{2Cd}{ip}}$$

Sometimes the EBQ is known as the Economic Order Quantity (EOQ).

For example, it costs £6 to place an order for an item costing £15. The company uses fifty a year and has an internal cost of capital of 10 per cent.

From the above, $C = 6$, $d = 100$, $i = 0.1$, $p = 15$

$$EBQ = \sqrt{\frac{2 \times 6 \times 50}{0.1 \times 15}} = \sqrt{400} = 20$$

The firm should buy the item twenty at a time.

6.9 Selling price

Imagine we are selling widgets for £18 when they cost us £15 to make. The marketing manager says if we increase the price to £21, we double our profit. Or do we? We certainly double the profit margin but probably at the expense of diminishing sales. If our sales plummet from 1,000 to 400, we shall see our total profit fall from £3,000 (£3 × 1,000) to £2,400 (£6 × 400). This is known as the law of diminishing returns.

Conversely, if we reduce the price to, say, £17, what affect will it have on sales? Suppose it increases them by 25 per cent. Our total profit again falls from £3,000 to £2,500 (£2 × 1,250). So the objective becomes finding the price which maximises profit.

[88]

If we were to plot a graph of total profit against price we would recognise it as a function like this:

$$P = xq - yq^2 \pm z$$

where P = profit, q = the order quantity, and x, y and z are unknown numbers which are found by plotting some sales figures on the graph (z does not need to be found).

By calculus we can determine that profit is maximised when:

$$q = \frac{x}{2y}$$

For example, a calculator's sales and costs per month are found to follow the formulae:

$$R = 200q - 4q^2$$
$$C = 40q + 100$$

where R = sales revenue for one month, and C = costs for one month.

From this we see that:

$$P = R - C = 160q - 4q^2 - 100$$

Profit is maximised when:

$$q = \frac{160}{2 \times 4} = 20$$

The sales price (S) of one item is:

$$S = \frac{R}{q}$$

In our example:

$$S = 200 - 4q = 200 - (4 \times 20) = 120$$

[89]

So the calculator should be sold for £120 at which twenty sales a month can be expected.

6.10 Modern measures

Many of the traditional management accounting measures given were formulated in the US before the war. Since then companies in some countries, notably Japan, have profited by concentrating on other figures.

These measures strike at the heart of the 'British disease'. In the UK we have become accustomed to first-class letters taking several days to arrive, companies taking at least a week to deliver when they have it in stock, and for products to go wrong and to take weeks to repair. Largely it does not occur to us as a nation that things should not be like that. As a writer, the only equipment I use is a word processor, telephone and fax machine. They have each gone wrong at least twice in their first year (are you reading this Amstrad, British Telecom and NEC?).

Japanese companies go for a *zero defects policy* – it is unacceptable ever to sell a defective product. Any defective product demands a full post mortem and a report to the chairman.

Such a policy can be sustained by measuring the *non-rework figure* – how many products are fully manufactured without any reworking. In the early 1980s directors of Hewlett Packard visited a Japanese factory where the non-rework figure was 92 per cent. When they measured their production, they found the figure was 8 per cent. Within 6 months this had been increased to 65 per cent and the rework staff had been cut by 25 per cent.

In production departments, things like setting up a machine have been regarded as fixed times incapable of improvement; every different job has had its own classification and stock inventories have had to be kept high to guarantee no stock-outs. Nissan honed down on all these areas; stock, for example, was ordered just 180 minutes before being needed on the production line. Try that with most UK suppliers!

The consequences of this can be shown by this comparison of two engine plants in 1982:

	Ford	Toyota
Output per employee per day	2	9
Factory space to make one car	777 sq ft	454 sq ft
Average life of stock inventory	3 weeks	1 hour
Number of labour classifications	200	7

It is easy to be cynical about such measures, particularly as Japan is not a popular country with many UK business managers, but such measures cannot be ignored for long by UK companies determined to succeed in the international market.

BANKING

7.1 Types of bank

The original function of a bank was just to provide a safe place where valuable items could be stored. Receipts or notes were issued for these items. Gold was often deposited and the receipts for this gold soon became such a convenient method of exchanging value that the notes were regarded as currency secured by the value of the gold denominated. Many banks still offer safe custody facilities, and the Bank of England and three Scottish banks still issues notes (though they are no longer exchangeable for gold).

Now the main business of banks has moved on to providing accounts and encashment facilities and to making loans. Banks are regulated by the Bank of England under the Banking Act 1987, which largely repealed the previous regulatory statute, the Banking Act 1979.

The term *clearing bank* is used to refer to those banks which are members of the cheque clearing system. In practice, this is now almost all of them. Sometimes the term *Big Four* is used in England to describe Barclays Bank, Lloyds Bank, Midland Bank and National Westminster Bank. The term *High Street bank* is another colloquialism used to denote the Big Four plus the Trustee Savings Bank, and Williams and Glyn's.

Commercial banks are those that specialise in meeting the needs of business, rather than in providing 'retail banking'.

Merchant banks are curious hybrid institutions. They combine some banking facilities with other services, such as commodity trading and underwriting. Traditionally there are two types of merchant bank. Accepting houses accept credits, while issuing houses underwrite and sponsor the raising of capital for business.

In recent years, building societies have been emancipated from their traditional roles and are now providing many services traditionally provided by banks.

7.2   Basic bank services

For the customer of retail banking, there are three broad services available:

1   funds management,
2   depositing money,
3   borrowing money.

These three broad services are respectively met by current accounts, deposit accounts and loan accounts.

Banks believe they have a right to charge twice for every service they provide. On a current account, the banks benefit from the (usually) free use of the funds you have. When you pay money into the bank, you are effectively making an interest-free loan to the bank. The banks also make charges for the various services they provide. Incredibly, they even charge you for making these 'interest-free loans' to them.

A deposit account pays interest at a much lower rate than that charged by the banks for borrowing from them. For instance, in November 1989 the bank rate was 15 per cent. It would be difficult for anyone to borrow money from a bank for less than 18 per cent (3 per cent above base rate). Yet the interest rates quoted for deposit accounts ranged from 5 per cent to 11 per cent (the top rate only offered by National Westminster Bank for investing £25,000 or more at 3 months' notice). These rates are paid after deduction of tax, and are therefore equivalent to 6.7 per cent to 14.7 per cent, still below base rate and way below the lending rate.

There are various types of loan account available, including revolving credits, which allow you to draw off money as

[93]

required. Again the banks expect to be paid twice for providing this service – by the interest charged and also on the 'arrangement fee'.

7.3 Cheques

A cheque is a written instruction to your bank to pay a sum of money to a person. For a cheque to be valid it must show:

1 a date,
2 an amount both in words and figures,
3 the name of the account against which it is drawn,
4 the name and address of the bank on which it is drawn,

and the cheque must be signed.

A cheque does not have to be written out from a chequebook or a form supplied by the bank. You can write a cheque on plain paper or indeed on anything else. Cheques have been written on paving slabs, dustbin lids, the side of a cow and on the midriff of a bikini-clad girl, usually either as a publicity stunt or protest.

A cheque does not have to be written on the date which appears on it. It can be postdated, but it must have a date. Strictly speaking, predating a cheque is a forgery offence.

Cheques are valid for 6 months, after which they go 'stale'. That does not end the payer's liability. If you find you have a stale cheque, you can demand that the person who wrote it pays you whatever he may still owe you. If you put the wrong year on a cheque, it can be stale immediately. However, over the New Year period so many people put the wrong year on their cheques that the banks will not regard such a cheque as stale.

A postdated cheque may only be paid in from the date written on a cheque.

Contrary to what many people believe, you can date a cheque on a Sunday. The only reason for not doing so is that such a cheque could be used as evidence of illegal Sunday trading.

7.3.1   *Cheques: amount*

The amount must be written in both words and figures, which must agree. If they do not, the cheque will be returned, except that if the mistake is only in the pence, the bank may pay the lower amount. For writing the words, it is usual to give the amount of pence in figures, e.g. 'one hundred and twelve pounds 16p', though the bank will accept a cheque written out for 'one hundred and twelve pounds sixteen pence'.

Cheques may be written in foreign currencies and will be converted to sterling by the bank.

7.3.2   *Cheques: signature*

When you open a bank account, you are asked to complete a form known as the mandate. This says who may sign the cheques. On a personal account you may want to allow your husband or wife to sign your cheques. A society or a company has to decide which officers may sign.

The mandate can also require more than one signature for certain cheques. For example, you may allow one of four people to sign up to £100, two people to sign up to £500 and one person and the chairman above £500.

A person who signs a cheque (or anything else for that matter) is called a signatory. The mandate must provide a specimen signature for each signatory, and the signatory must keep to that signature. If a signatory decides to change his signature, he must notify the bank on a new mandate and then only use his new signature.

A forged signature always makes the cheque invalid. If a bank pays out a cheque against a forged signature, it has to reimburse you the money, except if the bank can show that you were careless in some way. However, if you are unwise enough to sign a cheque without filling in the other details (known as a blank cheque) and someone fills in the details for their own benefit, you have no claim against the person who completed your cheque, or the person (payee) who received it.

[95]

7.3.3 Dishonoured cheques

If you have insufficient money in your account when your cheque is presented to the bank, the bank may dishonour the cheque. The bank must not pay part of it. For example, if you have £100 in your account and a cheque for £150 is presented to your bank, the bank can either 'bounce' the cheque or pay it, creating an overdraft of £50. In practice, most banks operate a 'shadow overdraft' system whereby customers are allowed to overdraw by a certain amount before the bank considers dishonouring the cheque.

If the bank bounces a cheque incorrectly, an action for libel may lie against the bank. For a business cheque, the damages can be substantial.

It should be noted that a person can sue against a dishonoured cheque under the Bills of Exchanges Act 1882. If you have simply not paid for goods supplied to you, there are many defences which could be advanced, such as the fact that the goods were defective or even not delivered at all. However, if you have issued a cheque, such defences are not available to you. The only defence is duress: in other words, you were forced to sign the cheque under, say, threat of violence.

7.4 Plastic money

'Plastic money' has come to refer to the various types of plastic card used instead of ordinary cash. There are five broad types of plastic money:

1 credit cards,
2 charge cards,
3 debit cards,
4 cash cards,
5 prepayment cards.

Credit cards allow you to make payment by signing a slip on which the embossed details of your card have been impressed. The banks again charge twice for the service. The shop where you buy the goods pays between 2 per cent and 5 per cent, and you pay interest on the amount borrowed after a period of between 2 and 6 weeks has elapsed. If the whole balance of the card is paid in this period, you pay no interest on the balance. There is a minimum balance which must be paid every month. The interest rates on credit cards are very high, usually up to twice the current bank base rate. The commonest credit cards are Access and Barclaycard, respectively part of Mastercard and Visa.

Charge cards work on a similar basis, except that the customer pays the whole balance at the end of each month. Instead of paying interest, you pay an annual fee. The main charge cards are American Express and Diners Club.

Debit cards automatically charge the balance to your account, using Electronic Funds Transfer at Point of Sale (EFTPoS) equipment. The card is 'wiped' through a machine which automatically debits your bank account. The first debit card was launched on 3 June 1987. The main debit cards are Connect and Swift. There is also a Visa debit card.

Cash cards operate machines in banks, allowing the holder to check the balance on his account and to withdraw amounts, usually up to £100 at a time. 'Smart cards', which incorporate a small microchip, are being designed for more sophisticated purposes.

Prepayment cards are bought to operate equipment. The card is then inserted to buy units of time. The commonest prepayment cards are phonecards issued by British Telecom and Mercury. A similar card is being marketed by Sky Television to unscramble its coded broadcasts.

Similar to these cards is the cheque card, which is not in itself a form of payment, but guarantees the payment of a cheque up to a set limit (generally £100).

Sometimes one card combines these functions. For example, a Barclaycard is a cheque guarantee card and a credit card; American Express, a charge card, may be used as a cheque guarantee card; and Lloyd's Bank offers one card which acts as a credit card, cash card and cheque card.

HIRING AND LEASING

8.1 Hire and hire purchase

Hiring and leasing are ways of enjoying the use of property without having to buy them.

Under the ordinary hire arrangements, you simply pay for the use on a time basis. The property is then returned. Under law, you have possession but not ownership.

A hire-purchase agreement is different. You hire the goods for an agreed period, and then make another payment to buy the goods. The period is sufficient to pay for the cost of the goods plus interest. For example, something costing £1,000 may have £200 interest added, which you pay at £100 per month. At the end of the period you pay a further sum, usually a nominal amount like £1, and the goods are then yours.

Hire-purchase agreements up to £15,000 are regulated by the Consumer Credit Act 1974 (and the mass of regulations passed under the provisions of this Act). The detailed provisions of the Act need not concern us here, as the hirer is obliged to tell you of them. Broadly the position is as follows:

1   You must sign in a conspicuous statement in a red box to acknowledge that you have been warned of the terms of the hire-purchase agreement.
2   The agreement must state the price of the goods, how much interest you are being charged and how many payments you must make before the goods are yours. It must also state the annualised percentage rate (APR) which you are paying (see chapter 3).

[98]

3   You can back out of the agreement at any time before the company decides to give you the credit. If the agreement was made 'off-premises' (i.e. at your home), you have a 'cooling-off period' of a further 5 days in which you may cancel the agreement. This is designed to protect people from high pressure doorstep sales techniques. If you cancel during the cooling-off period, you are liable to pay a £3 fee.

4   You must be given a copy of anything you sign at the time. If a hire-purchase agreement is concluded, a further copy must be posted to you within 7 days.

5   At any time, you may ask for a 'statement of payments'. The company may charge you a fee of up to 50p for providing this.

6   If the rate of interest is very high ('extortionate') for the circumstances, the court may reduce it. However, a rate of 48 per cent has been held not to be extortionate in a court case.

7   You may cancel the agreement at any time and send the goods back to the hirer. However, you must have paid up to half the price of the goods (and half the interest) and all your instalments must be up to date. If the goods have deteriorated beyond normal use, you are also liable to pay for any consequential loss of value.

8   You may pay off the hire-purchase agreement at any time. You are entitled to a rebate of part of the interest charge for early settlement.

9   If you fall into arrears on a hire-purchase agreement, the hirer can give you 7 days' notice to pay, failing which he may reclaim the goods. However, if you have paid more than one third of the credit price of the goods, the hirer must get a court order to repossess them.

8.2   Leasing

If you lease goods, they are never yours.

You pay lease rentals for a fixed period, usually enough to cover the cost of the goods plus an interest charge. This period is known as the primary lease period.

At the end of this period, you cannot buy the goods as is

normal for a hire-purchase agreement. Instead you move into a secondary lease period. This is an indefinite period where the lease rental is a nominal amount, usually a few pounds to cover the cost of paperwork.

An important practical difference between leasing and hire purchase arises on business assets. Any capital allowance available against tax may be claimed by a hirer of goods, but not by someone who leases them.

Goods which are effectively acquired under a lease must be shown in the accounts as if they were owned by the business, even though, strictly, the business does not own them.

If the asset leased is particularly large (in millions of pounds), it comes within the scope of *big ticket leasing*. This is a lease tailor-made for the asset. Such deals are usually arranged for a noticeably lower interest rate, usually below the bank base rate.

It is also possible to arrange a lease for less than the full value of the asset under *residual value leasing*. Under this the lessor effectively agrees to buy back the asset at the end of the primary lease period.

8.3   Credit-sale agreement

Another way of acquiring goods on credit is the credit-sale agreement. Under such an agreement, you acquire immediate ownership of the goods but are liable to pay a finance company for what is effectively a loan to buy the goods. The agreement for a credit-sale agreement must state this fact conspicuously in a red box which you must sign.

The laws for a credit-sale agreement are identical to those for hire-purchase agreements on such matters as documentation and the cooling-off period. However, there is no right to cancel the agreement and send back the goods; they are your propery. In addition, if you fall behind with the payments, the goods cannot be repossessed. The finance company can only start legal proceedings against you for debt in the usual way.

8.4   Faulty goods

If the goods you buy are faulty, you have a statutory right to have an immediate replacement at no extra cost to yourself. Note that you do not have a right to a cash refund, but neither do you have to wait for the goods to be repaired.

This provision still applies if some form of credit arrangement has been made to acquire the goods. However, in such circumstances you have extra protection in that you may make any claim against the finance company instead of the shopkeeper or supplier. This is useful if the supplier has gone out of business, cannot be found or is otherwise unable or unwilling to provide satisfactory redress.

This applies to all forms of credit purchase, including bank loans and credit cards. If you buy faulty goods with your Access card, you can require Access to make good your loss.

8.5   Guarantors

If approached by a friend, relative or colleague in connection with a credit application, you should be careful to establish whether you are being asked for a reference or a guarantee.

A reference is simply a statement of opinion about someone you know. Unless you are blatantly deceitful in your opinion (such as deliberately concealing knowledge of the person's fraudulant conduct), you risk no repercussions from providing the reference. However, if you provide a guarantee, you are underwriting the person's debt. If your friend (or whoever) defaults, you can be made to pay the whole amount he owes.

8.6   Credit references

Credit references are obtained by writing to a body which is licensed under the Consumer Credit Act 1974 to supply such information. There is no legal restriction on the person receiving the information, though the agency usually makes some requirements as a condition of supplying the information.

The information is purely factual. Generally it checks whether you are on the electoral roll, and records such things as bankruptcies and judgments registered against you. It may also record details of finance agreements which you have already made. Those who have previously supplied you with credit information may have entered details about you, particularly if you have been a slow payer.

It must be stressed that the credit reference agency does not decide whether you can or cannot have credit. It simply provides factual information against which the finance company (or whoever) decides whether to offer you credit facilities.

However you have the statutory right to know whether such an agency has been consulted, and, if so, its name and address. This applies whether or not the company has allowed you the credit facility sought.

You have the right to write to the credit reference agency, on giving your name and address and paying £1, to receive a full report of everything the agency has on file about you. This right may be exercised at any time. You do not have to wait until applying for credit.

If you believe the information held on file about you is wrong, you can require the agency to correct it. If it refuses, you have the right of appeal to the Director of Fair Trading.

8.7 Credit scoring

Credit scoring is a new departure in credit control. At its simplest the population is categorised according to over a 100 criteria. Your profile is then 'scored' according to certain parameters. From this you receive a score to indicate your creditworthiness.

This method is somewhat controversial for various reasons. First, it categorises you according to how people in your situation behave, which can be unfairly prejudicial. Second, some of the criteria can come near the limits imposed under sex and race discrimination laws. However, the companies insist that it is based more on your lifestyle and record than on prejudices, and that it considerably increases the accuracy of credit-granting.

9

INSURANCE

9.1   Types of insurance

Insurance can be obtained for:

1   life,
2   health,
3   house and contents,
4   public liability,
5   vehicles,
6   business.

There are also special policies for such things as ships, aircraft and the cancellation of public events. Indeed any unforeseen risk is, at least in theory, insurable.

Strictly speaking, insurance means that a payment is wholly dependent on a contingency, whereas assurance means that a payment is guaranteed. So cover against dying before age 65 is life *in*surance, whereas cover for death whenever it occurs is life *as*surance. However, these terms are now used more loosely and interchangeably.

Insurance is a contract effected by a policy for which you pay a premium. If the circumstances in the policy happen, you receive the sum assured.

It is essential to disclose all relevant facts when taking out an insurance policy or making a claim. You could find that your policy is invalid if you conceal or misstate information. In particular, it is often tempting to skimp on details about one's health record. Although extensive details are often requested, very few medical conditions (even serious ones)

[104]

are likely to lead to a refusal of cover or to an increased premium.

9.2 Life insurance

9.2.1 Types of policy

A life may be insured under various policies:

Whole life assurance insures you for death whenever it occurs.

Endowment assurance insures you for the earlier of death and a certain age. So such a policy for £100,000 aged 65 means that you will receive £100,000 when you reach 65, or your next of kin will receive £100,000 if you die before 65.

Pure endowment assurance insures you for survival to a certain date but not for death. Such a policy for £100,000 aged 65 means that you will receive £100,000 when you reach 65, but your next of kin will receive nothing if you die before.

Term assurance insures you against death in a fixed period. This policy has the advantage of being very cheap. For example, it may insure you against death in the next 10 years. If you survive those 10 years, you receive nothing.

Convertible term assurance insures you for death before a certain date, but has the option to convert to whole life or endowment assurance.

Joint lives assurance insures two lives on one policy. It pays out on either the first death (usually to the survivor) or on the second death.

Joint lives endowment provides an endowment on two lives. It pays out on a certain date unless one or both (as specified in the policy) people die before then.

Contingent survivorship assurance insures one life during another lifetime. For example, it may insure a husband's life during his wife's lifetime. If the wife dies before the husband, the policy pays nothing.

Deferred assurance provides cover *after* reaching a certain age. This is often used for children, providing cover after the age of (say) 21. If the child dies before the age of 21, no benefit is paid.

Issue risk policy provides insurance for birth rather than death. This policy is commonly used when someone will suffer loss if a child is born. An example is someone who will inherit money unless a closer relative is born.

9.2.2 Details of policy

As well as providing straight insurance cover, many insurance companies offer various ways of investing the funds to the policy holder's benefit.

The simplest of these is a *with profits* policy. The policyholder is entitled to a share of the profits made by investing his premiums. *Unit-linked assurance* is similar, except that the profits credited to the policy-holder are determined according to how units in a unit trust are doing, or according to an index.

Some policies are tailor-made to specific eventualities, such as providing school fees or maintaining a family income before children have left home. The amounts borrowed on mortgages are insured.

With *indexed* policies, the sum assured increases each year in line with inflation or some other index or measure. Sometimes the sum is increased automatically; sometimes you have to say whether you want it increased. The premium usually increases in line with the sum assured.

Convertible policies allow one type of insurance to be changed to another type.

Tax relief is given on life assurance polices taken out before 14 March 1984. This has the effect of reducing the premium payable (currently by 12½ per cent). The proceeds of life assurance policy are generally free of income tax. However, convertible policies issued after 24 February 1988 may be subject to income tax on their proceeds.

9.3 Health insurance

Health insurance protects people's income if they suffer illness or injury sufficient to incapacitate them from doing their normal work. This is an often ignored area of insurance.

In some age groups the risk of serious breakdown of health is fifteen times as great as death. If you are incapacitated rather than killed, there is a heavier burden on your finances. There is an extra person to feed, no life assurance proceeds and possibly additional expenditure to sustain you in your incapacity.

Premiums vary widely for this sort of cover, but typically a premium of about £350 will provide £1,000 a month for a 40-year old man, starting from his fourth month of incapacity.

Points to watch are:

1 The period for which payment is deferred. This may be 1, 3, 6 or 12 months. The longer the period, the lower the premium. The 3-month deferment period is common. As a rough yardstick, a 1-month deferment can double the premium. A 12-month deferment can halve it. It is always possible to have two policies with different deferment periods, so that some income starts after one month and extra income starts after 12 months.
2 Whether payment is made on prevention of your present occupation or on inability to follow any occupation. The former should normally be chosen.
3 Whether there is protection for a second period of incapacity within a period, and if so whether the deferment period has to start again. In other words, if you are off work for 4 months, and then after 3 months are off again for 6 months, for how much of that 6 months will you be paid?
4 The ability to increase your premiums without further medical evidence. The policy should allow you to increase your premium and cover year by year on an indexed basis, regardless of what subsequently happens to your health. Such policies are known as permanent health insurance.

9.4 Property

If you own a home, you should insure it and its contents.
Even if you lease or rent property, you may still be liable to
arrange such insurance.

Contents of a house should be insured for replacement
value. This is likely to be for much more than their cost or
value.

The house itself needs to be insured for rebuilding cost,
plus a sum (typically 10 per cent) to cover accommodation
expenses during rebuilding. The land itself does not need
to be insured. This arrangement is more expensive than
selling off the site for redevelopment, and is, frankly, a
poor deal for the householder, but that is the usual
requirement. The house should be insured for more than
the amount borrowed on the mortgage.

Insurance is against 'perils', certain predetermined
eventualities. The commonest peril for property is fire.
For contents, this is followed by theft. There are other 'all
risks' policies which provide cover for other eventualities,
such as accidental damage. However, even these usually
have some 'exclusions' – perils for which insurance is not
available.

Plate glass and sanitary fittings often need separate
insurance.

9.5 Public liability

Public liability is the responsibility to society in general.
This often arises from the ownership of property. For
example, you could be liable if a bird knocked a tile off your
roof injuring the postman.

Public liability insurance is often included with the
property insurance.

9.6 Cars

Since 1930 it has been a legal requirement that drivers of
vehicles are insured against death and injury to third
parties. This has been extended to include passengers. This

basic insurance does not insure the driver or the vehicle itself, nor does it cover damage to property (such as hitting other cars or demolishing a fence). EEC law is requiring this compulsory insurance to cover damage to third party property and to cover legal costs.

In practice the minimum insurance offered is 'third party, fire and theft'. This covers the legal requirements, and also insures the vehicle against damage by fire or theft (but not from other perils such as a 'hit and run' incident, though compensation may still be available from an agreement made by the Motor Insurers' Bureau).

The commonest insurance is comprehensive cover, which covers damage to the policy-holder's own vehicle.

9.7 Business insurance

A business has a need for additional insurance. All commercial premises, equipment and stock need insuring. There is usually a need for separate cover for goods in transit, and possibly also cash in transit.

Employees must be insured under the Employers' Liability (Compulsory Insurance) Act 1969, and a certificate to that effect must be conspicuously displayed.

Commercial vehicles need a different insurance policy from domestic cars.

Keyman insurance may be taken out on directors, senior managers and others whose death or absence would seriously affect the business. Keyman insurance is life insurance but where the company receives the proceeds.

There may be additional insurance for interruption to business to cover loss of profits while, for example, a burnt out factory is being rebuilt. Fidelity insurance can protect a business against defalcations of cash by members of the staff.

Debts may be covered by insurance or by some other arrangement, such as debt factoring. Overseas debts are usually insured through the Export Credit Guarantees Department.

Certain occupations have specific needs for insurance. For example, a manufacturer may have products liability insurance, a newspaper may have libel insurance, a hotel may insure its liabilities for loss of customers' baggage. Professional people have professional indemnity insurance. Farmers may have livestock and bloodstock insurance to protect horses, cattle and pigs against injury and disease.

9.8 Miscellaneous insurance

Almost any possible adverse risk may be insured against. New policies are always being devised.

It is common to have credit-card insurance to protect you against fraudulent use of your plastic money. Often the credit-card companies themselves include an element of insurance anyway.

You can have legal expenses insurance to cover you against the costs of a legal action. You can insure against having twins, against late departure of your holiday flight, and against rain when you get there.

PENSIONS

10.1 Introduction

Pensions are a means by which you put aside part of your income now, so that you have a source of income in your retirement.

You can receive pensions from three different sources:

1 the state,
2 company schemes (also known as occupational pension schemes),
3 personal schemes.

It is possible to provide for your retirement by saving. There are, however, two disadvantages in doing this. First, you will not benefit from the generous tax concessions enjoyed by pensions. Second, because interest rates are generally less than equivalent annuity rates, you will have much less to live on anyway.

10.2 Tax concessions

Pensions (other than state pensions) enjoy three main tax concessions:

1 your contributions are tax-deductible (up to a generous limit),
2 the pension fund itself pays no tax on its income,
3 any lump sum on retirement is free of all tax.

To qualify for all these benefits, pension schemes must meet strict conditions laid down by the state. Meeting these requirements is the responsibility of the pension fund, not you.

The law on pensions has changed many times, particularly since 1985. However, the tax concessions have remained largely unchanged since 1921.

Company schemes and personal schemes often provide a tax-free lump sum on retirement. State schemes do not. This lump sum is entirely free of all taxes. However, the regular weekly or monthly pension is taxed as if it were wages.

10.3   The state pension

The state provides both a basic pension and additional pension.

The basic pension is payable from 65 (men) or 60 (women) provided you have paid enough national insurance contributions. A woman may be entitled to a contributory pension on the basis of her husband's contributions.

Anyone whose working life has been spent in full-time employment, being unemployed or being self-employed is likely to meet this condition. Married women paying a reduced rate contribution, and anyone on a particularly low wage, may not need this requirement.

If insufficient contributions have been made, a reduced pension is paid. If not even a reduced pension is payable, a non-contributory pension (at a lower rate) is payable from the age of 80.

Before October 1989, the pension was reduced if the pensioner had earnings above £75 a week. This 'earnings rule' has now been repealed. Pensioners may earn what they like and still receive their full pension.

The basic pension can only be increased by being deferred, i.e. starting to draw it later than when you first become entitled. The increase is $\frac{1}{7}$ of 1 per cent for every week it is deferred from between 7 weeks and 5 years after entitlement. For a full 5-year deferment, the pension is increased by 37%.

The old age pension is paid at one rate for a single pensioner. There are additions for an adult dependant (such as a wife) or for having the custody of a child (not necessarily your own). These rates are fixed every year. The pension is taxed as if it were wages.

The non-contributory pension is a lower pension and is only paid from the age of 80. Your national insurance record is irrelevant. If you are receiving other benefits when you become 80, this pension may be reduced so that the amount you receive in pension and benefits is unchanged.

10.4   Additional pension

The additional pension is a further amount provided by the state according to the *amount* of your national insurance contributions. There are two types of additional pension:

1   graduated pension, and
2   SERPS.

10.5   Graduated pension

Graduated pension was paid by national insurance contributions between April 1961 and April 1975. Under the scheme, employees bought 'units' at the rate of one for every £7.50 (men) or £9.00 (women).

Each unit buys an amount of weekly pension expressed in pence. Although no further units can be bought, the values of the units already bought are increased annually in line with inflation. The value for 1991–2 is 6.81p a unit.

The maximum number of units someone could have is:

man (not contracted out)	86
man (contracted out)	72
woman (not contracted out)	48
woman (contracted out)	40

If you have units of graduated pension, you should have a notice telling you how many units you have.

10.6 SERPS

The State Earnings Related Pension Scheme (SERPS) started on 6 April 1978, and covers all employees who have not 'contracted out'.

Contracting out means that you are in a company pension scheme or have a personal pension scheme which is considered to be at least as good as SERPS (which is not difficult). A personal pension plan which contracts you out of SERPS is known as a Contracted Out Money Purchase Scheme (COMPS). SERPS provides an additional pension to those who retire after 5 April 1979. This is calculated as a percentage of average earnings (as defined).

In 1985 it was realised that the state could not afford the SERPS scheme as originally designed. At first, there was a suggestion simply to discontinue the scheme. However, it was eventually decided to let the scheme continue but on a reduced basis by making two basic changes:

1   with effect from 6 April 1999, average earnings will be determined over the whole working life rather than the last 20 years, and
2   between 1999 and 2010, the percentage applied to average earnings will be progressively reduced from 25 per cent to 20 per cent.

10.6.1   Band earnings

The pension provided by SERPS is calculated by references to 'band earnings', which are determined in two stages. First, you compare your actual earnings with the upper earnings limit (see below) for national insurance. You take the *lower* of these figures. Second, you subtract the lower earnings limit for national insurance. (If your earnings are less than the lower limit, your band earnings are zero.)

The upper and lower earnings limits since the introduction of SERPS are:

Pensions

Year	Lower limit	Upper limit
1991–2	£2,704	£20,280
1990–1	£2,392	£18,200
1989–90	£2,236	£16,900
1988–9	£2,132	£15,860
1987–8	£2,028	£15,340
1986–7	£1,976	£14,820
1985–6	£1,846	£13,780
1984–5	£1,768	£13,000
1983–4	£1,690	£12,220
1982–3	£1,534	£11,440
1981–2	£1,404	£10,400
1980–1	£1,196	£8,580
1979–80	£1,014	£7,020

10.6.2 Retirement before 1999

Someone who retires before 6 April 1999 will receive a SERPS pension based on the best 20 years' salaries. The pension will be 25 per cent of this average multiplied by $\frac{1}{20}$ for each year's contributions since 1979. So someone who retires in 1996 with 18 years' contributions and average earnings of £14,000 will receive an annual pension of:

$$25 \text{ per cent} \times \tfrac{18}{20} \times £14,000 = £3,150$$

10.6.3 Retirement after 1999

It is necessary to make separate calculations for someone who retires after 5 April 1999:

1 pension according to average earnings to 5 April 1998, and
2 pension according to average earnings from 6 April 1998.

For the former period, the average earnings are multiplied by the number of years worked in that period and divided by the number of years of working life. The SERPS pension for this period will be 25 per cent of the answer.

For the latter period, the average earnings are similarly

multiplied by the number of years worked in that period and divided by the number of years of working life. The SERPS pension for the second period is the answer multiplied by a percentage taken from the following table, according to the year of retirement:

Year of retirement	Percentage
1999–2000	25
2000–1	24½
2001–2	24
2002–3	23½
2003–4	23
2004–5	22½
2005–6	22
2006–7	21½
2007–8	21
2008–9	20½
thereafter	20

Example
A person retires in 2002–3 after 25 years' work. His uplifted average earnings for the period from 1978 to 1988 are £7,000. The equivalent average from 1988 to 2007 is £22,000.
His SERPS pension is:

$$25 \text{ per cent} \times {}^{10}\!/\!_{25} \times £7,000 = £700$$
$$23 \text{ per cent} \times {}^{15}\!/\!_{25} \times £22,000 = £2,530$$
$$\text{Total} \qquad\qquad\qquad\qquad £3,230$$

You can check your SERPS entitlement record with the DSS by handing in at any DSS office form BR 19 (which the office will provide), giving your name, address, date of birth and national insurance number.

10.7 Company pensions: overview

Company pension schemes, also known as occupational pension schemes, are run by an employer for the benefit of his staff. Strictly speaking, the scheme is run by an independent trust on behalf of the workforce. However, a scheme cannot be run unless the company agrees.

The scheme needs to be approved by the Inland Revenue for the employee to obtain the full range of tax benefits. In practice all company schemes are approved.

The scheme is either 'contributory' or 'non-contributory'. Under a contributory scheme the employee as well as the employer makes payments to the pension.

The scheme may also be either 'contracted out' or 'not contracted out'. This refers to whether the employee is a member of SERPS as well as the company scheme. Under a contracted-out scheme, the employee is not in SERPS, and both the employee and employer pay less national insurance. The scheme must provide a pension at least as good as SERPS (which is not difficult). This is known as the Guaranteed Minimum Pension (GMP).

Company schemes come under the statutory supervision of the Occupational Pensions Board (OPB). The tax aspects are administered by the Superannuation Funds Office (SFO), a department of the Inland Revenue which shares office space with the OPB.

A company scheme is almost always a 'final salary scheme' (also known as a defined benefit scheme), though it is possible for a company scheme to be a money purchase scheme, broadly similar to personal pension schemes. Company pensions usually provide other benefits, such as life insurance and widows' benefits.

10.8   Final salary schemes

Under a final salary scheme, your pension is found by multiplying your final salary (as defined) by a fraction. Such schemes usually provide for a lump sum, also calculated by reference to the final salary, as well as the pension.

The amounts depend on the length of the working life, relevant earnings and details of the scheme. The Revenue imposes a limit of $\frac{2}{3}$ final salary as annual pension and $1\frac{1}{2}$ times final salary as tax-free lump sum.

The final salary is usually calculated as the best of:

(a)   the last five years' salary, or
(b)   the average of the last three years' salary out of the last ten.

For schemes set up after 13 March 1989 and for members who joined existing schemes after 31 May 1989, the final salary is limited to £60,000 (which figure will be increased for inflation), limiting the pension to £40,000.

The fraction is usually $\frac{1}{60}$ or $\frac{1}{80}$ for each year's working life. Under a $\frac{1}{60}$ scheme, the maximum $\frac{2}{3}$ pension is possible after 40 years' working life.

Because few people are able to work 40 years, the Revenue allows the fraction to build up more quickly. From 1989, the full $\frac{2}{3}$ may be paid to anyone who retires between the age of 50 and 70 subject to 20 years' service. Schemes often allow people to buy 'additional years' to increase their pension.

10.9   Money purchase schemes

All personal pensions and a very few company schemes are money purchase schemes. Your contributions (and any from your employer under a company scheme) are allowed to accumulate in a fund with interest. At retirement the fund is then used to pay a lump sum and/or buy an annuity, according to prevailing prices at that time. An annuity is an arrangement where a lump sum is used to 'buy' income.

10.10   Lump sum

A tax-free lump sum payment may be paid on retirement under both company schemes and personal pension schemes. Under a final salary scheme, there is a limit of $1\frac{1}{2}$ times the employee's final salary. Within this limit, for retirement after 1989, the lump sum is the better of:

1   $\frac{3}{80}$ of the final salary for each year of service to a maximum of 40 years, and
2   $2\frac{1}{4}$ times the amount of pension before commutation.

[118]

For schemes submitted for automatic approval after 16 March 1987, the maximum lump sum is £150,000. For schemes set up after 13 March 1989 and for members who join existing schemes after 31 May 1989, the final salary is limited to £60,000 (which figure will be increased for inflation), limiting the lump sum to £90,000.

For a money purchase scheme, the limit is broadly one quarter of the fund.

There is no compulsion on anyone to take the lump sum. If you do, you will typically find that every £1 a year knocked off your pension produces a lump sum of £9 (man) or £11 (woman) at the age of 65; or about £11 (man) or £13.50 (woman) at the age of 60.

Example
A man with a money purchase scheme retires at 65 with a personal pension fund at £100,000, which will offer him a pension of about £11,000. He may take up to £25,000 as a lump sum payment. If he does, his pension will reduce to about £8,223.

10.11 Additional voluntary contributions

Additional voluntary contributions (AVCs) are extra payments made by an employee to a company pension scheme to provide additional benefits through the scheme. Under tax law, an employee may pay 15 per cent of his earnings into a company pension scheme. In practice, most employees pay much less. AVCs allow extra payments up to this 15 per cent limit to be paid into the scheme. So someone earning £12,000 a year and paying £600 a year into a company pension scheme, could pay up to an extra £1,200 in AVCs.

There are two types of AVC:

(a)   free-standing AVCs (FSAVCs), and
(b)   in-house AVCs.

FSAVCs are effectively separate little pension funds arranged by the employee independently of the company scheme. They have existed since 26 October 1987.

In-house AVCs are additional contributions to the main scheme. These have existed for many years, but it only became compulsory for companies to offer them from 7 April 1988. The company must offer the employee the choice of whether the AVC is used to buy extra years under a final salary scheme or more benefits on a money purchase basis. The company must also allow the employee some choice on how the AVC is invested.

AVCs may only be used to provide extra pension. They cannot increase the lump sum.

10.12 Company pensions: other benefits

A company pension scheme may provide other benefits up to certain limits.

It may allow for a widow's or widower's pension limited to two-thirds of the maximum lifetime income of the employee. If the person dies leaving no widow or widower, the pension may pay the benefit to another adult dependant.

If the employee dies leaving children, the scheme may pay them a pension, usually known as a 'children's allowance'. It is up to the scheme to decide what it counts as a child for these purposes, and even if it will make such payments anyway. The child must not be older than 21 unless in full-time education or training. The total of widow's/widower's pension and children's allowances must not exceed the amount of pension the employee would have received had he survived to normal retirement on his current salary.

Death in service benefit is limited to four times the employee's current earnings. Such a payment is free of all income tax and inheritance tax (except for controlling directors who die over 75 leaving no widow or widower).

10.16 Company pensions: leaving

If you leave a company scheme within 2 years of joining, you are only entitled to a refund of your own contributions. These are subject to income tax at 20 per cent. After 2 years' service, you may take a deferred pension or apply for the benefits to be transferred to a new scheme.

For employees who left after 1 January 1986, benefits accrued from 1 January 1985 must be increased annually by the lower of 5 per cent and the rate of inflation. Previously there was no requirement to increase the benefits at all.

From 1 January 1986, the employee has had the right under the Social Security Act 1985 for the benefit of one company pension to be transferred to another scheme. The transfer value is determined by a code of practice. This code is not neutral, in that you will still lose out by moving compared with staying in the previous employment. In addition, if you are on a higher salary as a result of the change of jobs, your pension entitlement will be proportionately reduced. Pension entitlement can be a very important factor in deciding whether it is worthwhile changing jobs, particularly in later life.

An employee has a further choice – to ask the trustees to buy out his pension entitlement by what is known as a 'section 32 annuity'. This is named after section 32 of the Finance Act 1981 (which is now section 591 of the Income and Corporation Taxes Act 1988). Section 32 annuities are also known as 'buy out bonds'. Since 1 July 1988, an employee may require his accrued benefits to be paid into a pesonal pension plan.

EMPLOYMENT

11.1 Wages

If you are employed, you are entitled to be paid wages or salary at a regular interval. Within 3 months of starting work, you should be given a contract of employment stating how much you will be paid, and when it will be paid (e.g. monthly in arrears) and how (e.g. by banker's order).

An employee does not have any automatic right to receive pay increases. These are a matter for negotiation between you (or a representative body such as a trade union) and your employer.

You are only entitled to commissions, bonuses or profit-sharing if this is specifically allowed in the contract of employment. Similarly you have no automatic entitlement to be paid for any overtime worked. If you are entitled to be paid for working overtime, this will be at your normal hourly rate of pay unless you have a specific agreement to be paid at another rate.

An employer is not allowed to pay different rates of pay to people according to their sex or race. Differentials should be based on other circumstances.

In some occupations there are minimum rates of pay laid down by Wages Councils.

11.2 Deductions

Your employer may only make deductions from your pay under the following circumstances:

1   when required by law, such as for income tax and national insurance,
2   when required by a court under an Attachment of Earnings Order (usually for the payment of a fine or an amount you have been sued for),
3   when requested by you (such as trade-union dues, pension-fund contributions or payroll giving to charity),
4   to cover shortfalls or deficiencies in the retail trade.

The last of these is perhaps the most controverial. If you are a shop assistant, barman or petrol station attendant, there can be discrepancies in the cash takings or stock during your shift. If your employer has sufficient evidence to prove that you appropriated the cash or stock, he can bring civil proceedings to cover them, or he can dismiss you on the spot and criminal proceedings may be started against you for theft. However, it is more likely that he can prove only that stock or cash was lost during your shift. The loss may be due to your carelessness rather than your dishonesty. For example, a customer may have shoplifted goods while your attention was distracted, or you may have given someone too much change.

In such circumstances, employment law allows your employer to recover the loss of cash or stock from your wages but only if this is specifically allowed in your contract of employment. There is a limit of 10 per cent of your pay which may be deducted. So if you earn £110 a week, and there was a £25 deficit on your shift, your employer may only deduct £11. The other £14 may be deducted from subsequent payslips but always within the 10 per cent limit. Any uncleared balance may be deducted in full from your last payslip.

An employer is not entitled to make other deductions. For example, if you refuse to pay for a canteen meal or goods brought from a staff shop, the employer cannot deduct the money from your payslip.

Every time you are paid you are entitled to receive a payslip, showing the gross and net amounts of your pay and detailing all deductions. Every year you receive a form P60, detailing your gross earnings, tax and national insurance. When you leave, you receive two parts (of three) of a P45 tax certificate stating how much you have earned since the beginning of the tax year (6 April) to the date of leaving, how much tax has been paid and what tax code has been used.

11.3   Holidays

There is no law allowing any employee to have any holidays at all. Entitlement is governed entirely by the contract of employment. Even if holidays are allowed, there is no law requiring you to be paid for them. Again, entitlement to holiday pay is determined according to your contract of employment.

It is normal to allow employees paid leave on the eight public holidays and for so many other 'working days' each year.

11.4   Sickness

If you are sick while employed, you may be entitled to statutory sick pay (SSP) from your employer. If you are not entitled to SSP, you may be entitled to sickness benefit from the DSS.

In addition, your employer must pay any sick pay allowed in your contract of employment (occupational sick pay). The employer may also make voluntary payments if he so wishes.

You are entitled to statutory sick pay if you are an employee aged between 16 and retirement age. You are not entitled to SSP if:

1   your contract of employment is for a fixed period of less than 3 months (unless you have actually worked 3 months),
2   you are on strike or engaged in any industrial dispute,
3   you have not actually done any work for your employer,
4   you are working outside the EEC,
5   you have already been paid 28 weeks' SSP in that tax year,

[124]

6   you are claiming statutory maternity pay.
7   your earnings are less than the lower earnings limit for
    national insurance (£46 a week for 1990-1).

There are a few other circumstances when SSP is not
paid.

SSP is generally paid from the fourth day of sickness until
you return to work (or leave, die or retire, if earlier) to a
maximum of 28 weeks. If you have a second absence for
sickness within 8 weeks of a previous one, you are paid
from the first day of the second absence.

Sickness is any mental or physical condition which stops
you doing work you can reasonably be expected to do. So if
you are a storeman and break a leg, you are 'sick' only if
there is no part of your job you can do while your leg is
broken. If, for example, you can be fully engaged on
sedentary work (such as paperwork) which is part of your
job, you cannot claim to be sick.

Sickness also covers:

1   precautionary absence, e.g. to stop a pregnant woman
    contracting rubella from a colleague,
2   convalescence certified as necessary by the doctor, and
3   absence while you are a carrier of an infectious disease.

It does not cover compassionate leave, e.g. a single
parent staying off work to look after a sick child.

There are two rates of SSP, depending on your average
weekly earnings.

The employer will state what notification and evidence
he requires to pay SSP. He can only insist on a doctor's
certificate from the eighth day of absence. If there is any
dispute between the employer and employee, the matter
may be referred to the DSS.

If you are sick, but are not entitled to SSP, you may be
entitled to sickness benefit instead. This is a contributory
social security benefit paid by the DSS. Sickness benefit is
paid for 28 weeks starting from the fourth day of illness on
terms broadly similar to SSP.

If you are still sick when the 28 weeks' period has expired, you automatically receive invalidity benefit. This comprises a weekly 'pension' regardless of age, and an allowance (additional to the pension) if you are under 60 (man) or under 55 (woman). This continues until you return to work, reach retirement age or die.

The employer may make different conditions for paying occupational sick pay. For example, he may not pay occupational sick pay for sporting injuries but be willing to pay for compassionate leave.

Sickness benefit and invalidity pensions are tax-free. Invalidity allowance is taxable. Statutory sick pay and occupational sick pay are subject to income tax and national insurance.

11.5 Maternity

A woman who has been employed for at least 26 weeks is entitled to statutory maternity pay (SMP), with a few exceptions. SMP is administered in a way very similar to SSP. The employer reclaims SMP and SSP from the state.

If the employee has worked for at least 16 hours a week for 2 years, or for at least 8 hours a week for 5 years, she is entitled to SMP at a higher rate. This is 90 per cent of her normal weekly earnings for the first 6 weeks, and a fixed rate for the following 12 weeks. If she has been employed for 26 weeks but is not entitled to the higher rate, she receives the lower rate of allowance, which is the fixed rate for 18 weeks.

The length of service is determined at the point 15 weeks before the expected birth. The 18-week period of SMP starts between 6 and 11 weeks before the expected date of birth.

If the pregnancy ends more than 12 weeks before the expected date of birth other than in the birth of a live baby or babies, no SMP is payable. Otherwise, SMP is fully payable, even if the baby is stillborn.

If a woman is not entitled to SMP, she may be eligible for maternity allowance. This is a contributory social security payment paid by the DSS for 18 weeks, starting from the eleventh week before the expected date of birth. A woman on low income may also be entitled to a maternity grant (£100 for 1990–1) from the Social Fund.

A pregnant employee who has been employed for at least 2 years generally has the right to return to work within 29 weeks of leaving, providing she gives notice before leaving. Giving notice does not commit her to coming back.

A woman is entitled not to be dismissed just because of her pregnancy. She is also entitled to paid time off for ante-natal care.

Maternity is not a sickness, and therefore no sickness payments arise during a normal maternity. However, if the pregnancy, childbirth or childcare leads to illness or injury to the mother, sickness payments are payable, subject to the usual rules.

There are no rights for payment or paternity leave for fathers. It should be noted, however, that EEC regulations are more generous on maternity and paternity provisions, and this may become reflected in UK law.

11.6 Redundancy

If you are made redundant after more than 2 years' service, you are generally entitled to redundancy pay. Note first that redundancy means that the employer has contracted his business in the area where you are working. Changing working methods so that you are no longer needed is not in itself redundancy. The point is a fine one, but can be important. If redundancy is not the real reason for dispensing with your services, you may have an action for unfair dismissal.

If you are fairly made redundant, you are entitled to so many weeks' pay in addition to your normal pay. Your weekly pay up to a certain limit (£172 a week for 1989–90) is multiplied by 1½ for each year's service while you were over 40, by 1 for each year's service while you were between 22 and 40, and by ½ for each year's service between the ages of 18 and 21. You can go back up to 20 years. These amounts are reduced if you are made redundant in the year before retirement.

[127]

Example
A man aged 43 is made redundant after 22 years' service.
His weekly pay is £150. His redundancy pay is:

$$3 \times 1\frac{1}{2} \text{ weeks} = 4\frac{1}{2} \text{ weeks}$$
$$\underline{17} \times 1 \text{ week} = \underline{17 \text{ weeks}}$$
$$20 \text{ (max)} \qquad 21\frac{1}{2} \text{ weeks}$$

$$21\frac{1}{2} \times £150 = £3,225 \text{ redundancy pay.}$$

Redundancy pay is free of tax and national insurance. The employer is free to pay you more as a 'golden handshake', which is usually tax-free up to £30,000.

11.7   Strike action

Employment law has many specific provisions regarding industrial action, which basically means refusing to do what you are contracted to do or being prevented (by a lock-out) from doing so. For financial purposes, working to rule, refusing to work overtime and generally being uncooperative do not comprise industrial action.

The consequences of industrial action are:

1   you are not entitled to any pay (though the trade union may pay you strike pay),
2   the period of taking action does not count towards your period of continuous employment for determining such matters as unfair dismissal and redundancy. If you take action in your first year of employment, the whole of that first year is excluded from the reckoning.
3   you are not entitled to receive any tax refunds under the PAYE system (these are kept until you return to work),
4   you and all your fellow strikers may be dismissed, but if the employer dismisses only some of the strikers, they have a claim for unfair dismissal,
5   you are barred from claiming income support (a social security benefit) for yourself and if you make a claim for benefit to support your family, the DSS will assume that

you are receiving £17.50 a week strike pay (whether you are or not),
6   you cannot claim statutory sick pay or statutory maternity pay, nor start an action for unfair dismissal.

In 1990 it is proposed to bring in a law to allow an employer fairly to dismiss a worker who organises a strike not officially sanctioned by a recognised trade union. Such strikes are usually known as 'wildcat strikes'.

12

INSOLVENCY

12.1 Legal nature

Insolvency is the inability to pay your bills as they fall due. In itself, this has no legal consequences at all. If your creditors (the people to whom you owe the money) are prepared to wait or reach an agreement with you, there is no further legal problem.

However, if you owe £750 or more and your creditor is not prepared to wait and you cannot come to some agreement, the creditor may then petition for your bankruptcy. There are other grounds which may also be used to support a bankruptcy petition, but this is the commonest ground.

Even if you are in this unhappy position, the creditor may still be unwilling to petition for your bankruptcy. The court fees and legal expenses can be high. Although these are also claimable from you, you are only liable to the limit of your wealth. The creditor cannot get blood out of a stone.

Bankruptcy law is designed to achieve a fair balance between the creditor's right to his money and the unfortunate's 'right' to be given a second chance. The law has become easier on the bankrupt since the nineteenth century, when a debtor was held in prison indefinitely, and fed on bread and water until he paid. Whether the law is fair to the parties is a matter still hotly debated to this day.

Under a bankruptcy, most of your property is sold to pay off your creditors. Any uncleared balance is then wiped out. While you are an undischarged bankrupt, there are some restrictions on what you are allowed to do financially.

Eventually (usually after 5 years), you can be discharged. You can then start again, poorer, but with no debts.

Major debts, such as house mortgages, are usually 'secured loans'. This means that if you default, the lender may take over named property, e.g. by repossessing your house. This does not in itself make you bankrupt. However, such action may prompt your other creditors to take action.

12.2   Stages of bankruptcy

The presentation of a bankruptcy petition against you in itself has no legal significance. If the court is satisfied that the petition is justified, a receiving order is made. Your property passes into the possession and control of the Official Receiver (a government appointee). However, you remain the legal owner of the goods. The electricity, gas, water and telephone companies are told. They may require you to have a slot meter fitted (where possible).

The Official Receiver then interviews you in private about your personal affairs. He then invites each of your creditors to submit a 'proof of debt'. From this he produces a 'statement of affairs' – an account of how much you have and how much you owe. He also checks to see if you have committed any fraud (which would support criminal proceedings) and if you have any money or assets squirrelled away, perhaps with friends or relations, or under a false name.

He must also call a meeting of your creditors. You can propose a 'scheme of arrangement' for dealing with your debts. For example, you may propose paying one quarter of them in each of the next 4 years. The creditors are then asked to vote on whether they will accept your scheme. The scheme must involve paying at least 25 per cent of the debt, and be supported by at least 50 per cent of the creditors by number, and 75 per cent of the creditors by value.

From this, you may have to submit to a public examination. This is held in open court, open to the public, and can be a most embarrassing and humiliating experience. You are under oath and can be required publicly to answer very personal questions.

The court then decides whether to make an adjudicating order. This order makes you bankrupt. A trustee is appointed (usually an accountant). He sells most of your possessions to pay your creditors.

Note that bankruptcy is a personal incapacity. If you are married, your bankruptcy does not similarly affect your husband or wife. For example, the matrimonial home cannot usually be taken from your husband or wife unless they are also bankrupted. But do not rely on this. The general rule is that the home should be sold and half paid to the spouse. The exception to this rule is not always applied.

Attempts to avoid the effects of bankruptcy by transferring property to your husband or wife can usually be frustrated. The trustee has wide powers to reverse 'gifts' in such circumstances.

12.3 Being bankrupt

All a bankrupt is allowed to keep is:

1 necessary bedding and clothing, and
2 tools of his trade up to £250 in value.

However, property owned by someone else of which he has use is not affected.

As a bankrupt, you suffer these disadvantages:

1 you cannot obtain credit (or try to obtain credit) for more than £50 without disclosing that you are an undischarged bankrupt,
2 you cannot be a company director, or take part (directly or indirectly) in the formation, management or winding up of a company,
3 you cannot hold public office, such as being a magistrate, MP or local councillor, and there are similar bars in other walks of life, e.g. an accountant who is adjudged bankrupt is automatically struck off.

You are registered as bankrupt with the main credit

reference agencies. Thus anyone who checks your bankruptcy will know the position.

There are certain restrictions on your ability to trade. You must either use your pre-bankruptcy name or trade name, or must tell everyone that you are an undischarged bankrupt.

If you open a bank account, you must tell the banker that you are an undischarged bankrupt and give the name of the trustee. The bank must notify the trustee (who usually orders the account to be closed).

All money you receive from any source is automatically passed to the trustee, who only allows you to have the minimum needed for basic support, not for luxuries. The trustee cannot, however, touch your pension fund. He can deny you funds to continue making contributions to it, and can take any payments you receive from it by way of pension or lump sum, but the pension fund itself remains out of his reach.

12.4   Order of payment

There is an order for paying your creditors, which is broadly as follows:

1   pre-preferential creditors (basically the expenses of the trustee and his staff),
2   secured creditors (those who lent on the security of a particular asset, such as the house or car),
3   preferential creditors (basically 1 year's tax, 6 months' VAT, employees' wages up to £800 per employee, national insurance on employees' wages, and rates or community charge),
4   ordinary creditors (other people to whom you owe money and who are not deferred creditors),
5   deferred creditors (basically business partners and interest on debts).

If there is still any money left over, it is paid to you. You are still bankrupt, but have an excellent case for applying for a discharge.

The classes outlined above are paid one at a time in that order. So if the money runs out paying the preferential creditors, the ordinary creditors will receive nothing. If an ordinary creditor instigated the bankruptcy proceedings, not only will he be out of pocket for his original debt, but he will be out of pocket for the legal expenses as well.

If there is not enough to pay all the creditors of a class, they receive an equal proportion, known as a dividend. For example, if ordinary creditors are owed £120,000 and only £12,000 is available for them, they will each receive a 10 per cent dividend.

12.5 Discharge

After a period, a bankrupt may be discharged. This means that he is free from all disabilities attaching to bankruptcy. The slate is wiped clean (apart from tax arrears and affiliation payments), and he can freely trade, take credit, own property and generally assume normal life again.

After the public examination, the court will decide whether the provisions for automatic discharge are to apply. This allows the bankrupt to be automatically discharged after 5 years. The decision depends on the bankrupt's conduct. One who became bankrupt from gambling and womanising, who fraudulently hid his assets and destroyed documents, and who was unco-operative with the Official Receiver, is not likely to be automatically discharged. Someone who became bankrupt only because of the unexpected failure of a reasonable commercial venture and who co-operated fully is likely to receive an automatic discharge.

Otherwise a discharge is granted on the bankrupt's petition, which may be submitted any time after the public examination. The court may authorise an unconditional discharge. Alternatively it may allow a conditional discharge, whereby conditions are imposed on the bankrupt. For example, it may seem appropriate to allow a person to trade without the stigma of bankruptcy and to pay off some arrears by instalments. The third option is a suspended discharge, which takes effect from a future fixed date or when a certain dividend has been paid to creditors.

12.6 Companies

A company is not bankrupted. It follows a different procedure, laid down under company law.

In outline, the company may go into receivership or liquidation. The receiver is a 'doctor' who saves what he can of the company, perhaps by selling bits of it off to other companies who can manage it better. Sometimes a receiver can keep the whole company intact and turn it round just by doing a better job than the previous managers.

A liquidator is an 'undertaker'. His job is to sell off all the assets for the best price he can to pay the creditors. A liquidator is not basically interested in saving the company as a trading organisation.

If the company is not saved, it is then 'wound up'. The consequences of winding up are that the company ceases to exist. It is effectively killed off.

The general rules about creditors' meetings and ordering of debts are similar as for bankruptcy.

MISCELLANEOUS

13.1 Financial planning

Financial planning is a fairly new discipline which looks at your personal circumstances as a whole. For example, a financial planner is unlikely to recommend a large amount of life assurance for a single person living on his own. Who needs the money when he dies? The planner is more likely to recommend that you have generous health insurance, to provide an income on incapacity.

The elements of financial planning are basically:

1 Budgeting – keeping your expenditure within your income.
2 Establishing an emergency fund (typically of 2 or 3 months' income) to cope with the unexpected. The emergency fund is usually kept in a bank deposit account or a building society.
3 Being insured in all proper areas.
4 Having adequate pension arrangements.
5 Making suitable investments.
6 Tax planning. Tax avoidance is the legal arrangement of your affairs to minimise your tax liability. It should be distinguished from tax evasion, which is the illegal falsification or concealment of your affairs to the tax authorities. Tax planning is the process of tax avoidance.
7 Estate planning – making a will, making sure that your beneficiaries know where to find all your property, and planning for inheritance tax (usually by setting up trusts).

13.2 Investments

13.2.1 Golden rules

Money is invested to provide a 'return'. This usually comes from two sources: regular payments (such as dividends or interest), and the profit expected when the investment is sold. However, many investments only offer one of these sources.

There is now a bewildering array of investments which can easily confuse you. The following points about investment should be noted.

1 You should only invest money after you have established an adequate emergency fund.
2 Do not borrow money to invest. The rate of return is unlikely to exceed the interest in your borrowings. Similarly, be careful of investing earmarked money. If you are investing in shares, a good return can depend on selling the shares when you want to. Having to sell them, to pay for your holiday or a daughter's wedding, can reduce the return.
3 Only invest in what you understand. If moving into a new type of investment, try a 'dry run'. This is where you pretend to invest and monitor the theoretical performance. Then only invest a part of your available capital. Some investments benefit from acquiring a specialist knowledge. This certainly applies to investments in shares, and even more so to investments in collectibles, such as coins and stamps.
4 Generally the greater the return, the greater the risk. You may find that you have a choice between an absolutely guaranteed return of 10 per cent (from a building society, for example), or a 1 in 10 chance of a 200 per cent return, failing which you receive nothing (say from a traded option).

   The degree of return and risk which is acceptable to you depends on your personal circumstances. Even high risk investments need not necessarily be like gambling on the horses. For example, if you buy ten traded options as described above, you have an average chance of a 20 per cent return over all and a negligible chance of losing the lot. Similarly, some high risk investments can be used to minimise other investment risks. For example, a put option on the FT-SE index can reduce the downside risk of owning ordinary shares, but remember only to invest in what you understand.

5 Only deal with reputable people. Deal with a High Street bank, a member of the Stock Exchange, or someone recommended by them. Alternatively, ask your solicitor or bank manager for advice on someone offering their services to you. Banks and stockbrokers are bound by a code of ethics and supported by 'lifeboats' to provide funds to repay you should they sink with your cash. Other investment managers may not have this protection.

6 Resist all high pressure sales techniques. If a deal cannot stand scrutiny and deliberation, it is probably dodgy. Many 'special offers' on timeshares in Spain or for obscure overseas companies are dodgy in the extreme; also beware of mysterious investments that appear to defy normal financial principles.

13.2.2 Risk

At its simplest, the following gives an order of risk for different types of investment, starting with the safest (which usually have the lowest returns):

1 National Savings and gilts. You know exactly how much you will receive and when, and your funds are guaranteed by the government.

2 Premium bonds. Your investment is guaranteed by the government. However, your return is decided by chance (about 11,000 to 1 for a single bond). If you have a large enough holding, this averages out to a fairly reliable and acceptable interest rate from the smaller prizes (which account for about 98 per cent of the prize money), plus you have the chance of winning a big prize.

3 Building society and bank deposit accounts. It is most

unlikely that your capital will be lost and there are lifeboats to protect your funds even if they were. The interest rates vary.

4   Unit trusts and investment trusts. It is possible to lose some of your capital if the investment does badly, but for most trusts even a 20 per cent loss is unusual. Interest rates vary according to how the company does.

5   Ordinary shares, and stock. It is possible to lose some of your capital if the company does badly. Public companies rarely go bust (which would result in your shares losing all their value), but a 50 per cent loss is not unknown. The return depends entirely on the company's fortunes, without the benefit of being offset by spreading the risk over various companies, as unit trusts do.

6   Traded options. Here you are not buying shares, but buying or selling the right to buy them at a set price by a set date. If the price moves the wrong way, you lose the whole investment. If it moves the right way, you can make a fortune.

7   Financial futures. Here you are entering into a contract to buy or sell shares at a future date. If the price moves the wrong way, you could not only lose your entire investment, but be forced to pay up many more times the amount to honour your contract. Commodity dealing and foreign currency speculation have a similar very high risk profile.

13.3   Trading organisation

If you are setting up in business, you must choose what type of trading organisation to be. Basically, the question is whether to 'incorporate', which means setting up a limited company.

The advantages of incorporation are perpetual succession and limited liability. A limited company is a separate legal body from you, and continues after you have died. Similarly, you can sell it, or some of it, to someone else. Limited liability means that the company can only be made to pay what the company owns. Your own property and wealth cannot be touched.

The disadvantages are that it costs money to be registered. Every year you must pay an auditor, and must file accounts and pay a fee. There are also heavier record-keeping burdens.

Usually the best plan is to start as a sole trader and incorporate later. There can be considerable tax savings in doing this, as a sole trader can pay tax on his earnings much later than a company.

The advantages of a limited company are of little value in the early days. If the company is worth little, its rights of succession are not of much consequence. Similarly, if there are few debts, limited liability is not much advantage either. For early debts, such as bank loans, mortgages and property rental, you will probably be asked to give personal guarantees anyway.

INDEX

Index

[143]

UNDERSTANDING FINANCE

Public liability insurance, 108
Public sector borrowing requirement, 48
Public spending, 48
Puffins, 5
Punts, 4
Purchase day book, 73
Purchasing power, 40
Pure endowment assurance, 105

Qualified audit report, 80

Rates of income tax, 24
Real terms, 64
Realisation of profit, 74
Receivership, 135
Recovery, overhead, 83
Redundancy, 127
References, credit, 101
Registration for VAT, 34
Residual value leasing, 100
Retail price index, 38
Retained profit, 71
Retirement pensions, 111
Retirement relief, 27
Return and risk, 137
Revaluation, 78
Revolving credits, 93
Risk in investing, 138
Roll-over relief, 28
Rule of 72, 59
Rule of 97, 34

Sales day book, 73
Scheme of arrangement, 131
Scottish notes, 2
Second-hand VAT schemes, 33
Section 32 annuities, 121
Secured creditors, 133
Secured loans, 130
Selling price, optimum, 88
SERPS, 114
Shadow overdrafts, 96
Share premium, 71
Shortfalls (wage deduction), 122
Sickness pay, 124
Signatures on cheques, 95
Silver coins, 6
Simple interest, 55
Single Administrative Document, 35
Sources of taxable income, 19
Special drawing rights, 16
Spot rates, 16
Stamp duty, 30
Stamp duty reserve tax, 31
Standard time (management accounting), 82

Standards, accounting, 77
State earnings-related pension scheme, 114
State pension, 112
Statement of affairs, 131
Statements, 77
Statements of recommended accounting practice, 78
Statements of standard accounting practice, 77
Statutory maternity pay, 126
Statutory sick pay, 124
Sterling index, 51
Stock valuation, 78
Strike action and pay, 128
Surplus, 75
Synthetics, 82

Tariff Codings, 36
Tax and prices index, 53
Tax concessions of pensions, 111
Tax-free income, 20
Taxes, 18
Term assurance, 105
Third party motor insurance, 109
Top-slicing relief, 23
Traded options, 139
Trading organisation, 139
Translation, 15
Troy weight, 53

Undischarged bankrupts, 130
Unemployment, 53
Unit trusts, 139
Unit-linked policy, 106
Units of graduated pension, 113
Upper earnings limit, 115

Valuation of assets, 78
Value added tax, 31
Variance analysis, 83
VAT number, 34
Visible trade, 46

Wages, 122
Wages book, 73
Whole life assurance, 105
Widow's bereavement allowance, 22
Widows' pensions, 120
Winding up, 135
With profits policy, 106
Women as taxpayers, 22

Zero defects policy, 90
Zero-rating, 33